CELPIP
focus

LISTENING and SPEAKING

CELPIP Focus: Listening and Speaking

In response to ongoing research and development, changes may occasionally be made to the CELPIP Test. There may be short periods of time when study materials do not exactly match the current official test format, and content may be updated to match changes to the CELPIP Test without prior notice. Check celpip.ca for any updates to the CELPIP Test.

Copyright © 2018 Paragon Testing Enterprises, a subsidiary of The University of British Columbia

Paragon Testing Enterprises, Vancouver, British Columbia, Canada

First Printing: October 2018
Second Printing: March 2019

ISBN 978-1-988047-28-7

CONTENTS

The CELPIP Test
About the CELPIP Test

The Canadian English Language Proficiency Index Program (CELPIP) is a computer-delivered general English language test administered by Paragon Testing Enterprises, a subsidiary of The University of British Columbia. The CELPIP Test measures how well test takers can communicate in English in a variety of social, workplace, community, and daily life situations. The format and scoring of the test are referenced to the Canadian Language Benchmarks (CLB).

The CELPIP Test is offered in two versions. This chart summarizes the main features of each version.

CELPIP–GENERAL TEST			CELPIP–GENERAL LS TEST		
✓ Four-skills test			✓ Two-skills test		
✓ About 3 hours			✓ About 1 hour 10 minutes		
Listening	6 parts*	47–55 minutes	**Listening**	6 parts*	47–55 minutes
Reading	4 parts*	55–60 minutes	**Speaking**	8 tasks	15–20 minutes
Writing	2 tasks	53–60 minutes			
Speaking	8 tasks	15–20 minutes			

* There may be additional unscored items in the Listening and/or Reading Tests which are used for research and development purposes. See celpip.ca for more information.

Tip Doing a CELPIP Practice Test is a great way to familiarize yourself with test features and get ready for your test day. You can access free practice test questions and purchase practice tests at celpip.ca.

How to Use This Book

This book is divided into two modules, Listening and Speaking. Each unit within a module is independent of the others, so you can do them in any order. Since the skills get harder to master as you work through the module, it is easier to start at the beginning of the module and work through the units in order.

Features

Look for the icons shown below to quickly locate specific features.

LISTENING SKILLS:
These skills help improve your ability to get the score you need on the Listening Test.

SPEAKING SKILLS:
These skills help you perform at your best on the Speaking Test.

ACTIVITY:
These are practice opportunities for the skill you are learning. Answers, some with explanations, are provided in the Answer Key.

ONLINE RESOURCE:
This icon indicates that there are resources on the internet that will be needed for the activity.

TIP:
These are important tips and strategies to improve your performance on the test.

NOTE-TAKING:
This feature shows ways to set up your notes for each Listening part.

The Modules

The Listening Module

- The format of the six parts of the Listening Test is explained.
- The different kinds of questions found on the Listening Test are discussed.
- Each unit explains either a single Listening part, or multiple Listening parts that share similarities.
- An infographic shows key elements and computer navigation features for the Listening Test.

The Speaking Module

- An overview of the test component explains the format of the Speaking Test and gives information about performance expectations.
- Each unit explains a single Speaking task.
- An infographic shows key computer navigation features for the Speaking Test.
- Sample responses have been provided for each task in the Speaking Test.
- Speaking tasks are presented as they look on the test screen.

Each unit focuses on key language skills and essential test-taking strategies. A complete Answer Key is included, with explanations for some activities. The speaking checklists will help you assess your Speaking responses.

Accessing Media and Transcripts

This book uses numerous audio and video files to support the skills and activities that are discussed. To access this media, please go to the Focus LS Resource Portal (link below) and click on the matching filename. Full transcripts are also provided for relevant media clips.

Online Resource: https://secure.paragontesting.ca/ip/focus-ls

For Instructors

Use this book to build your own CELPIP test preparation course. The activities here are best suited to self-study, but many can be adapted for working in groups of two or more. Here are a few suggestions to get you started:

- Students can work in pairs to complete an activity.
- Students can complete an activity alone and discuss their answers in small groups.
- After completing an exercise, students can exchange books and mark each other's answers.
- Students can provide feedback on each other's Speaking responses using the speaking checklists in Units 7–14.
- To make full use of this book, you may wish to access the media for the class, as well as project the relevant transcripts.

UNIT 1

Overview of the Listening Test

LEARNING FOCUS

- Format of the Listening Test
- Understanding question format
- Identifying question types
- Previewing
- Improving your listening

The Listening Test consists of a variety of typical daily social and workplace situations. This includes conversations, news items, reports, and discussions in which people express different viewpoints. Before listening to the audio in each part, you will see a brief statement providing some context about what you are about to hear. You will be required to listen for information, infer meaning, identify main points and important details, and perform other listening tasks as you complete each part of the test.

In this unit, you will become familiar with the overall format and the different types of questions you will find on the Listening Test. Knowing what to expect on the Listening Test can make a big difference in your performance.

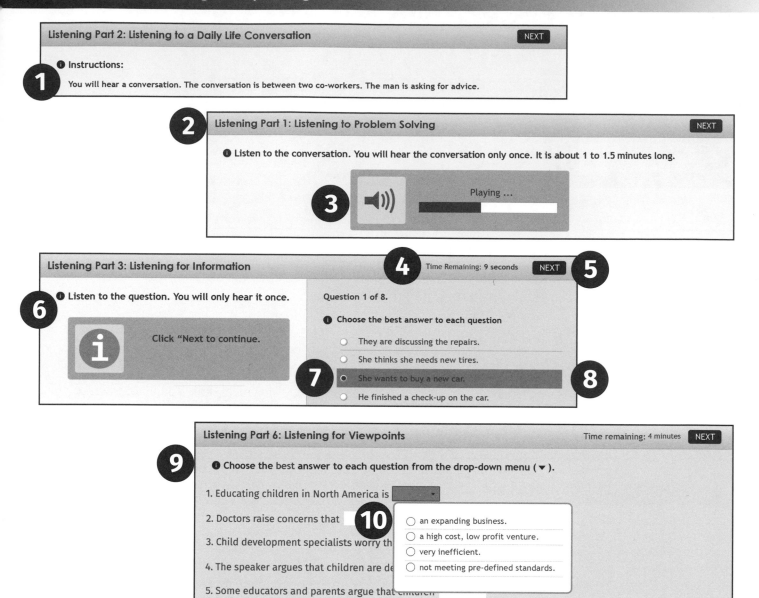

① The prelistening statement helps give context before the audio or video starts.

② The title reminds you where you are in the test.

③ The audio or video plays on this page, and the blue bar shows the progress of the audio clips.

④ The countdown timer shows how much time you have left for this page. When the timer reaches zero, the test will move to the next part.

⑤ Use the NEXT button to move to the next part before the timer reaches zero. You cannot move back.

⑥ The audio will play ONCE for each question in Parts 1–3. You will only hear the questions—you will not see them.

⑦ Click on the circle to select the best answer. Change the answer as many times as you like.

⑧ In Parts 1–3, each screen displays answer choices for a single question.

⑨ All the questions are displayed on the same page in each of Parts 4–6.

⑩ Click on the box to see the answer choices.

Format of the Listening Test

There are six parts to the Listening Test, as well as an unscored practice task at the beginning. There may be additional unscored items which are used for research and development purposes. You will have about 50 minutes to complete the Listening Test. The test is computer scored and it gets more difficult as you work through it.

LISTENING PART	TASKS
Listening to Problem Solving	Listen to a dialogue between two people, divided into three parts, and answer questions.
Listening to a Daily Life Conversation	Listen to a dialogue between two people and answer questions.
Listening for Information	Listen to a dialogue between two people and answer questions.
Listening to a News Item	Listen to a news story and answer questions.
Listening to a Discussion	Listen to and watch a discussion between three people and answer questions.
Listening for Viewpoints	Listen to a report containing multiple perspectives and answer questions.
TOTAL TIME	**About 50 minutes**

Understanding Question Format

All questions that may appear on the Listening Test are multiple choice, and there are two different styles, shown below.

1) **Sentence-Completion Questions**
   Choose among four ways of completing a single sentence.

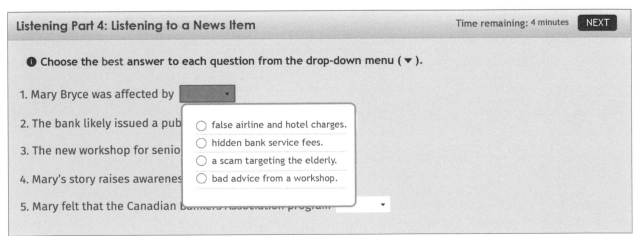

Listening Part 4: Listening to a News Item — Time remaining: 4 minutes — NEXT

ⓘ Choose the best answer to each question from the drop-down menu (▼).

1. Mary Bryce was affected by [▼]
2. The bank likely issued a pub[ ]
3. The new workshop for senio[ ]
4. Mary's story raises awarenes[ ]
5. Mary felt that the Canadian b[ ]

○ false airline and hotel charges.
○ hidden bank service fees.
○ a scam targeting the elderly.
○ bad advice from a workshop.

2) WH Questions

Answer questions that begin with words like "what," "when," "where," and "why." The options for these answers may be presented as text or, in Listening Part 1, as images. The questions themselves are given as audio only in Parts 1–3, and as text only in Part 5.

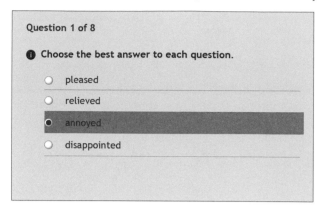

For the question above, you would hear, "What is the man's reaction to the woman being in his yard?"

For the question above, you would hear, "What did the woman likely have in her hand?"

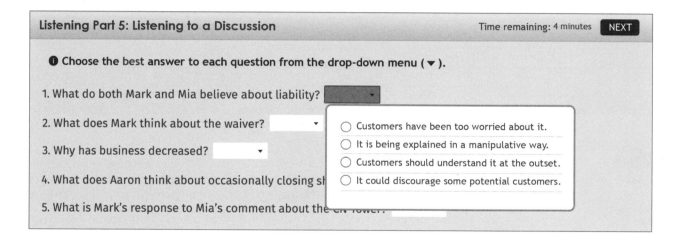

For the question above, you would hear... *(as shown in image)*

Identifying Question Types

Questions for the Listening Test can be grouped into three types.

1. GENERAL MEANING	2. SPECIFIC DETAILS	3. INFERENCE
• These are questions that focus on understanding the overall idea in a passage. • You may be asked to identify the topic, theme, or main idea of a Listening passage.	• These are questions that focus on understanding specific details in a passage. • You may be asked to identify key information, supporting details, opinions, or examples.	• These are questions that focus on drawing conclusions and making assumptions based on information in a passage. • You may be asked to identify implicit information, including a speaker's purpose, tone, or attitude.

Activity 1

Listen to the audio taken from Listening Part 1, and then read the questions below. You do not need to actually answer the questions.

> Play **Unit 1 - Track 1.**
> Access the audio via the Focus LS Resource Portal; the link is found in the Introduction.

1. What is the problem?

2. Why will the woman go to the cab driver?

3. Why is the woman so upset?

Identify the question type for each question above.

QUESTION NUMBER	QUESTION TYPE
1	
2	
3	

Previewing

When each Listening part begins, start by previewing the screen to check for key information.
- Determine how many speakers there are.
- Identify the context.
- Check how many sections each audio passage has.
- Check how long each audio section is.

Activity 2

Scan the following images and answer as many questions as you can below. Note that not *all* questions may be answerable from the given information.

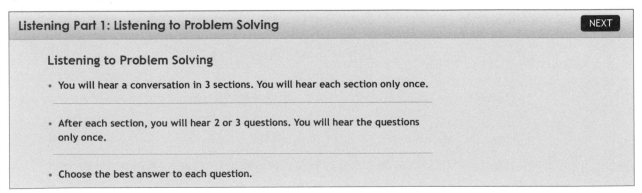

Listening Part 1: Listening to Problem Solving   NEXT

Listening to Problem Solving

- You will hear a conversation in 3 sections. You will hear each section only once.

- After each section, you will hear 2 or 3 questions. You will hear the questions only once.

- Choose the best answer to each question.

Listening Part 1: Listening to Problem Solving NEXT

ⓘ **Instructions:**

You will hear a conversation between a woman and a man. The man is an employee at a store and the woman is a customer.

Listening Part 1: Listening to Problem Solving NEXT

ⓘ **Listen to the conversation. You will hear the conversation only once. It is about 1 to 1.5 minutes long.**

Playing ...

1.

   a) What will you hear?

   b) How many speakers are there?

   c) Where are the speakers?

   d) How many sections will the audio have?

   e) How long is the audio?

Listening Part 2: Listening to a Daily Life Conversation | NEXT

Listening to a Daily Life Conversation

- You will hear a conversation followed by 5 questions.

- Listen to each question. You will hear the question only once.

- Choose the best answer to each question.

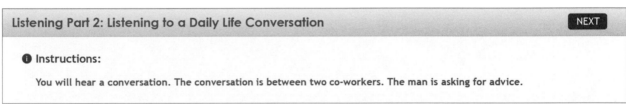

Listening Part 2: Listening to a Daily Life Conversation | NEXT

ⓘ Instructions:

You will hear a conversation. The conversation is between two co-workers. The man is asking for advice.

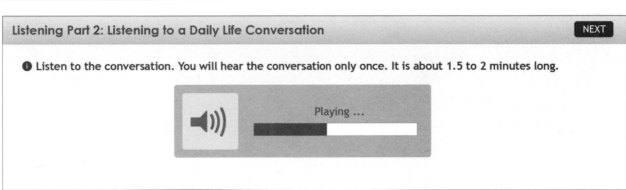

Listening Part 2: Listening to a Daily Life Conversation | NEXT

ⓘ Listen to the conversation. You will hear the conversation only once. It is about 1.5 to 2 minutes long.

Playing ...

2.

a) What will you hear?

b) How many speakers are there?

c) Where are the speakers?

d) How many sections will the audio have?

e) How long is the audio?

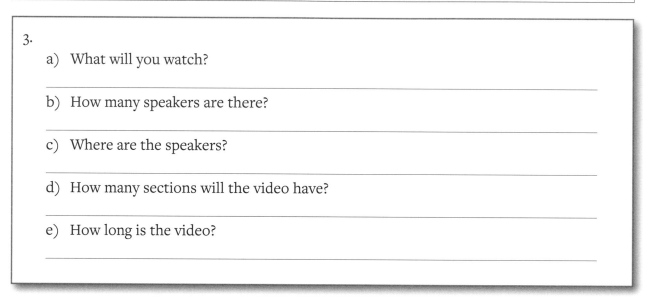

Listening Part 5: Listening to a Discussion `NEXT`

Listening to a Discussion

- You will watch a 2-minute video. Then 8 questions will appear.

- Choose the best way to answer each question.

Listening Part 5: Listening to a Discussion `NEXT`

ⓘ **Instructions:**

You will watch a discussion between three co-workers. You will be introduced to them at the beginning of the video. There are two men and one woman. They are colleagues at a rollerblade rental shop.

3.

    a) What will you watch?

    b) How many speakers are there?

    c) Where are the speakers?

    d) How many sections will the video have?

    e) How long is the video?

Improving Your Listening

In preparing for the Listening Test, there are various ways to improve your skills. Try to set aside some time each day, even if it's only a few minutes, to listen to the news or audiobooks, or to watch movies or television. You could also listen to people around you. Listening to a variety of material will help you increase your range of vocabulary, idioms, and expressions. The Canadian Broadcasting Corporation (CBC) website is a great place to start. Most importantly, listen to audio and watch videos that interest you. This will make your listening practice much more enjoyable, and you may learn new words and phrases.

UNIT 2

Listening to Conversations between Two People

LEARNING FOCUS

- Understanding Parts 1–3
- Identifying the relationship between the speakers
- Following a sequence of events
- Understanding conversational English
- Note-taking
- Test practice

The first three parts of the Listening Test share a few similarities: they include conversations between two people about a topic common to daily life, and you must answer multiple-choice questions. There are also some important differences between these Listening parts. In order to best illustrate these similarities and differences, Listening Parts 1, 2, and 3 are addressed together in this unit.

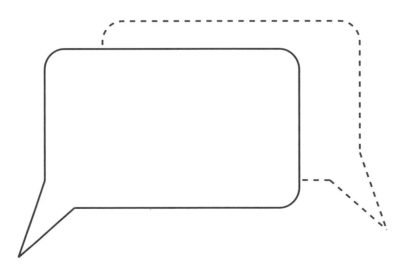

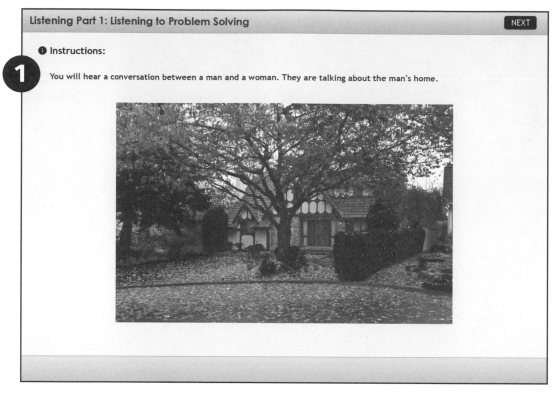

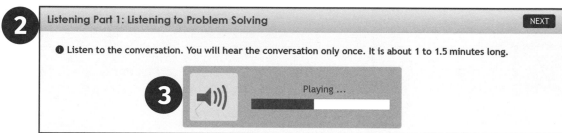

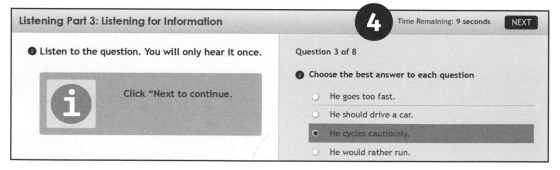

① The prelistening statement in Part 1 includes text and an image. Parts 2 and 3 only include text.

② The Part 1 conversation audio has three sections; conversations in Parts 2 and 3 have one section each.

③ In Parts 1–3, you will only hear the questions—you will not see them. The number of questions varies between parts.

④ In Parts 1–3, you will have 30 seconds to listen to each question and select an answer.

Understanding Parts 1–3

Part 1: Listening to Problem Solving is a conversation between two strangers in which one has a problem, and the other is trying to help him or her solve the problem. This conversation is split into three sections, each followed by a few comprehension questions. To answer these questions, you need to understand the basic facts, opinions, and details. Sometimes you will need to make inferences.

In Part 2: Listening to a Daily Life Conversation, you will hear a conversation about a day-to-day activity or workplace situation. To answer the questions that follow the conversation, you need to understand the basic facts, identify paraphrases, and make note of changes in topic. You may also need to make inferences.

Part 3: Listening for Information contains a conversation where an expert is giving information that is unfamiliar to the other speaker. To answer the questions following the conversation, you need to listen for key information, understand inferences from facts and evidence, and connect ideas.

When you listen to conversations on the street, at home, or in CELPIP Listening Parts 1, 2, and 3, it's helpful to identify whether the speakers know each other and what role or position they have. Another skill you will need is to be able to follow the course of the conversation and understand how ideas are connected to each other.

Identifying the Relationship between the Speakers

When listening for the relationship between speakers in a conversation, there are two things to be aware of. The first is their roles, and the second is how well they know each other.

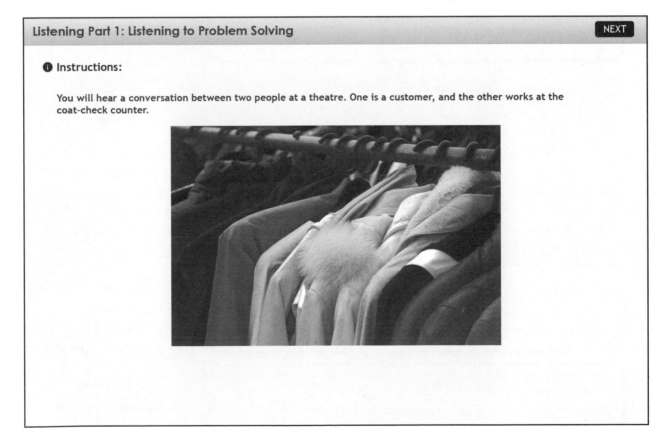

Listening Part 1: Listening to Problem Solving   NEXT

ⓘ Instructions:

You will hear a conversation between two people at a theatre. One is a customer, and the other works at the coat-check counter.

Identifying Roles

There are two steps in identifying the role each speaker plays. The first is to preview and identify the roles as described in the information screen (see previous image).

Then, listen to the audio, paying special attention to information that will further develop your understanding of the speakers' roles. Read the following excerpt from a conversation and note the key words and phrases that will help you infer the relationship between the speakers.

Man: Hey, Laura. If you have a minute, I've got something I'd like to ask you about.

Woman: Sure. What's on your mind? Do you have more relationship questions? That's what we usually talk about.

Man: Not this time. This is a work thing. You know our boss has been working for the company for a long time, right? Well, he's retiring next month, and since he's always been so good to me, I'd really like to get him a retirement gift.

This comment about *"our boss"* and *"the company"* shows that the speakers are co-workers.

Woman: That's a great idea. Wait a minute; usually all the employees get together to buy a gift. Why are you buying him a gift on your own?

The idea that the speakers are co-workers is confirmed by the fact that the woman identifies both herself and the man as being among the *"employees"* that *"usually get together to buy a gift."*

Identifying Familiarity

The other method for identifying the relationship between speakers is analyzing the level of familiarity. Familiarity between speakers is shown through the way they talk. In general, when people are familiar with each other, they tend to use less formal language; when two strangers interact, they are likely to use more formal expressions. Below are three excerpts from listening passages that demonstrate how the speakers' words show what kind of relationship they have.

Excerpt One

Man: Okay, ma'am, your car's ready. Everything mechanical checked out fine. I noticed that you've still got winter tires on your car. Are you going to change them?

By using the polite term *"ma'am,"* the man is indicating that he does not know the woman.

Woman: Seriously? I just bought this car, and it passed a safety inspection. What's wrong with the tires?

Excerpt Two

Man: Hey, how's it going? Have you heard the news? Josh's gonna get into uni after all. He actually passed that crazy hard exam.

By using slang like *"how's it going"* and informal contractions/abbreviations like *"gonna"* and *"uni"* for *"going to"* and *"university,"* it is clear that the man is friends with the woman. If they weren't friends, the use of the slang might be inappropriate.

Woman: Seriously? That's sweet! Good for him!

Excerpt Three

Man: Hey, Laura. If you have a minute, I've got something I'd like to ask you about.

By calling the woman by her first name, the man is demonstrating that there is some level of familiarity.

Woman: Sure. What's on your mind? Do you have more relationship questions? That's what we usually talk about.

As discussed previously, these two speakers have been identified as co-workers. In addition to this, the woman's question shows that the connection between the speakers is close, since good friends talk about relationships.

Activity 1

Listen to the audio and answer the questions below.

Play **Unit 2 - Track 1.**
Access audio via the Focus LS Resource Portal; the link is found in the Introduction.

1. How many speakers are in the passage? _____

2. What is the relationship between the speakers?
   a) They are strangers.
   b) They are co-workers.
   c) They are classmates.
   d) They are friends.

3. Are the speakers familiar with each other?
   a) Yes
   b) No

Following a Sequence of Events

Being able to follow the flow of ideas in a conversation is a key language skill. There are a number of ways to keep track of the connection between ideas. One way is to pay attention to the pronouns used. In the first speech bubble below, the woman replies that "it wasn't my cup of tea, to be honest." This requires you to understand that "it" refers to the word "performance" in the man's question. Linking pronouns to the correct nouns referred to earlier in the conversation is an important part of understanding what is happening in a listening activity.

Man: Hello there! How was the performance?

Woman: It wasn't my cup of tea, to be honest. I guess I don't really like musicals.

Man: Oh, that's too bad. Well, I'll get your jacket for you. Could I have your number please?

Woman: Yes, it's just in my pocket . . . here it is, it's #240.

Man: Thanks. Just a minute . . . Um . . . ma'am . . . I'm sorry, what does your coat look like again?

Woman: Why do you ask? It should be on the hanger with the matching number. It's a black parka jacket with grey fake fur on the hood.

→ **Time**

Activity 2

Use the excerpts in the speech bubbles above to answer the following questions. Write your answers in the blanks provided.

1. In the phrase "Oh, that's too bad," what does "that" refer to? _____

2. In the phrase "Yes, it's just in my pocket," what does "it" refer to? _____

3. In the phrase "It should be on the hanger with the matching number," what does "it" refer to? _____

Activity 3A

Using what you have learned about following a sequence of events, listen to each track and decide which of the two excerpts ("A" or "B") come next in the conversation. Write your choice in each box.

Play **Unit 2 - Track 2.1.**

A. Man: The other attendant went home sick. It's just me. I understand you're upset, and I'm very sorry, but if you could just come back in 5 minutes. If we can't find it, I'll call my supervisor.

B. Man: Yes, I will, but if you could just wait a few minutes. There are many other people waiting in line. I'm sure I'll be able to find it once I clear more coats.

1. _____

Play **Unit 2 - Track 2.2.**

A. Woman: Oh, thank goodness. Where was it?

B. Woman: But I already called a cab! It's probably waiting outside for me! Can someone else check it for me?

2. _____

Play **Unit 2 - Track 2.3.**

A. Woman: I certainly hope these mix-ups don't happen too often. Perhaps I should complain to your supervisor.

B. Woman: Oh—Well—Thank you very much!

3. _____

Play **Unit 2 - Track 2.4.**

A. Man: And we do hope you'll buy tickets for another show some time!

B. Man: I'll call you another one, and it will be paid for by the theatre company.

4. _____

Activity 3B

Now that you have worked on the conversation in Activity 3A, listen to the audio and answer the questions below.

Play **Unit 2 - Tracks 3.1–3.11.**

Play **Track 3.1**	Listen to the first part of the conversation.			
1. Play **Track 3.2**	a) He is simply trying to be polite. b) He is collecting data for a survey. c) He was unable to watch it himself. d) He was an actor in the performance.			
2. Play **Track 3.3**	a)	b)	c)	d)

Unit 2 – Image 1: This image is not displayed in full colour. See the original image online in the Focus LS Resource Portal.

Play **Track 3.4**	Listen to the second part of the conversation.
3. Play **Track 3.5**	a) Someone has spilled tea on her coat. b) The attendant cannot find her coat. c) There are two identical winter coats. d) One ticket number goes with two coats.
4. Play **Track 3.6**	a) The coat was very expensive. b) It is very cold outside. c) She is very fond of the coat. d) The coat is irreplaceable.
5. Play **Track 3.7**	a) He wants to call the other attendant for help. b) He wants to deal with the other customers. c) He wants to call his supervisor for instruction. d) He wants to give her time to calm down.
6. Play **Track 3.8**	a) to ask the cab driver to wait for her b) to look in the cab for her missing coat c) to return home in the cab right away d) to wait inside the cab for 5 minutes

Play **Track 3.9**	Listen to the third part of the conversation.
7. Play **Track 3.10**	a) Another employee put the woman's coat on the wrong ticket. b) Another employee mistook the woman's coat for her own. c) The woman's coat looked like the one hanging beside it. d) The woman's coat was hidden from view by other coats.
8. Play **Track 3.11**	a) He gives the woman free tickets for a show. b) He offers to have the coat cleaned. c) He says he'll file a complaint with the supervisor. d) He arranges for the theatre to pay for her cab.

Bookend Statements

Another way to connect ideas is to listen for "bookend" statements. These appear at the open and close of a conversation and serve many purposes. The first is to set the tone of the conversation. For example, if a speaker begins a conversation with an angry tone and then slowly becomes more neutral, you could infer that the other person is helping with the problem. The tone can also help you clarify whether the speakers know each other, since people use different tones for strangers or friends. For example, strangers may speak to each other with a fairly neutral tone, while people who are more familiar with each other may speak with more emotion.

Another purpose of a "bookend" statement is to frame the context of the conversation. If you take the information in the opening and closing statements, you will probably be able to understand the basic situation: what happened and how it concluded. Opening statements usually involve a greeting and introduce the action, whereas closing statements usually involve a farewell and a final reference to what was discussed.

Play **Unit 2 – Track 4** and read along with the transcript below.

> MAN: Excuse me, could you please tell me what you're doing in my front yard?

> WOMAN: I'm sorry, I didn't think anyone was home. I'm the townhouse gardener. We're doing assessments of what trees need to be pruned or removed.

(The bulk of the conversation has been removed.)

> MAN: That's great! Did you speak with the neighbours as well?

> WOMAN: I did. And they agreed that, for the shade, it's worth keeping the tree.

> MAN: Terrific! Thanks so much!

> WOMAN: No problem. Have a nice day!

In this example, only a few sentences are given. However, the main idea of the conversation is clear. Initially, the man seems bothered by the woman in his yard, as expressed by his frustrated tone. The woman is a gardener and she is checking the trees. Between these "bookends," there was a problem, but from the closing statement, it is evident that the problem was solved. This is indicated by the speakers ending the conversation with a positive tone.

Activity 3C

Practice identifying "bookend" statements by reading the following and labelling each set as either "opening" or "closing."

1. _____	Woman: You'd think they could have used dark green at least, not blue! Man: Maybe they didn't have dark green either. Woman: True. Anyways, it works, that's all that matters. Thanks for your help!	2. _____	Man: Hi, how can I help you? Woman: Hi. I'd like to exchange my backpack. The strap broke. I can only carry it on one shoulder now.

Now that you are familiar with how to identify opening and closing "bookends," these next two activities will expand this idea further.

Activity 3D

Listen to the audio and write the track numbers for each opening and closing pair on a line below.
Play **Unit 2 – Tracks 5.1–5.4.**

Track 5.1	Track 5.2	Track 5.3	Track 5.4

OPENING	CLOSING

Activity 3E

Listen to the audio and write the track numbers for each opening and closing pair on a line below.

Play **Unit 2 – Tracks 6.1–6.6**.

Track 6.1	Track 6.2	Track 6.3	Track 6.4	Track 6.5	Track 6.6

OPENING	CLOSING

As demonstrated in these activities, clues to the main ideas of a passage can often be determined from the opening and closing statements. Being able to follow along with the ideas in a conversation like this is important on the CELPIP Test. Sometimes you might be asked a question that requires you to understand how the conversation developed and if a topic was the main idea or a small detail.

Understanding Conversational English

One of the greatest challenges in listening to English is clearly identifying what is being said when the speakers use **contractions** and **interjections**.

Contractions are made by joining words to make language more efficient. These are some of the most common contractions:

- it's = it is
- didn't = did not
- aren't = are not
- we've = we have
- you're = you are
- we're = we are
- they're = they are
- I'd = I would OR I had
- she's = she has OR she is

It is important to understand the context of how the contraction is being used, especially because some contractions can have multiple meanings.

Interjections are commonly used in two ways. Sometimes interjections are used to express emotions ("wow," "oh my," and "thanks"). Interjections are also used when people do not know what to say next ("um," "uh," and "ah").

Activity 4

Listen to the audio and then complete the table by writing each contraction you hear in the order that you hear it on the left side. After listening, write the full words on the right (You've → You have). Some contractions will appear more than once.
Play **Unit 2 – Track 7**.

CONTRACTION	FULL WORDS
1.	
2.	
3.	
4.	
5.	
6.	
7.	
8.	
9.	
10.	
11.	
12.	
13.	
14.	
15.	
16.	
17.	
18.	
19.	
20.	
21.	
22.	
23.	
24.	

Note-Taking

Being able to take notes is a key skill that helps when participating in business meetings, classroom lectures, and other information-heavy conversations. This skill is also useful when completing the Listening Test in CELPIP. On the official test, you will be provided with a pen and notepaper, in case you wish to take notes while listening to the passages. It is your choice whether you take notes or not. At the end of the official test, all notepaper will be collected, but you will not be scored on your notes.

Whether you use the following strategies or not, keep in mind that it doesn't matter how many notes you take or whether they contain any spelling or grammar mistakes. Only you will see them, so as long as they make sense to you, that's good enough.

Two of the most important strategies for note-taking are using symbols or shortened words, and organizing the notes so that the information is easy to locate. These strategies will be discussed in more depth in the following activities. Keep in mind that you may also wish to draw diagrams, free-form images, or even use emoticons in your notes. Ultimately, you should take notes in whatever way you find to be the most efficient.

Symbols and Shortened Words

This list contains some of the most common and useful symbols used in note-taking. This list is **not** exhaustive.

♀		woman, women, female
♂		man, men, male
a.m.		morning
p.m.		afternoon
NB	*	note well (from the Latin "nota bene"), remember this, important
w/		with
w/o		without
⟹	∴	therefore, consequently
∵		because
approx.	≈	approximate(ly)
=		equals, is the same as, results in

Access the Focus LS Resource Portal for additional materials.

Using shortened words can make the note-taking process more efficient. Three methods are listed below.

Remove vowels
- garden   →   grdn
- government   →   gvrnmnt
- people   →   ppl

Replace letters with an apostrophe (')
- thinking   →   think'g
- respond   →   resp'd

Use the first three letters of a word
- government   →   gov
- March   →   Mar
- contradict   →   con

Organizing Notes

There is a wide range of note-taking methods; one such method is speaker-based organization.

Speaker-based organization focuses on each speaker and asks WH questions such as: Who is the speaker? Where is the speaker? What is the speaker doing? When is the speaker doing this? Why is the speaker doing this? Sometimes, there is no direct answer to these questions, but thinking about them will help you focus on important information. To take notes in this style, take a sheet of paper and divide it into sections. You will need one section for each speaker.

SPEAKER 1	SPEAKER 2
Who:	Who:
What:	What:
When:	When:
Where:	Where:
Why:	Why:

Before you hear the conversations in Listening Parts 1, 2, and 3, you will be presented with a prelistening statement that will give you information about the speakers. For example, the prelistening statement may be, "You will hear a conversation between a man and a woman." Based on this information, you can begin to fill in the chart by identifying the gender of each speaker in the "who" section of the chart as soon as the audio starts.

Activity 5

Listen to the audio and practice taking notes. Then compare your notes with the sample notes in the Answer Key.
Play **Unit 2 – Track 8**.

LISTENING NOTES	
SPEAKER 1	**SPEAKER 2**
Who:	Who:
What:	What:
When:	When:
Where:	Where:
Why:	Why:

Test Practice

Using everything you have learned, play the following tracks and choose the best answer for each question.
Play **Unit 2 – Tracks 9–11**.

> **Tip** In Listening Parts 1–3 on the official test, you will only be able to hear the passage and questions **once**. In preparation for this, try to listen to each track only once as you answer these questions.

Listening Part 1: Listening to Problem Solving

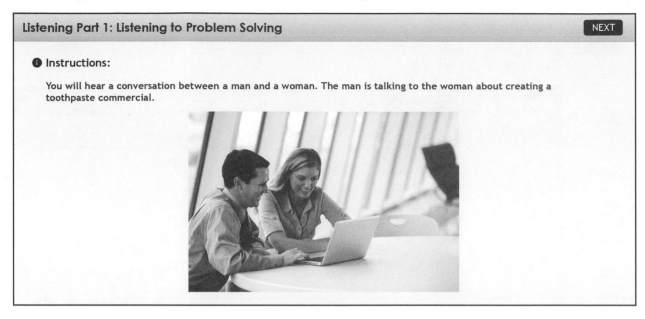

Play **Track 9.1**	Listen to the first part of the conversation.
1. Play **Track 9.2**	a) They need to reduce expenses. b) They need more time to finish. c) The script needs to be changed. d) The deadline has been moved up.
2. Play **Track 9.3**	a) b) c) d)

Unit 2 – Image 2: This image is not displayed in full colour. See the original image online in the Focus LS Resource Portal.

Play **Track 9.4**	Listen to the second part of the conversation.
3. Play **Track 9.5**	a) Pleasing her client is important to her. b) She doesn't like last-minute changes. c) Spending too much on actors worries her. d) She has an uptight attitude.
4. Play **Track 9.6**	a) reducing the actors' salaries b) hiring new script writers c) making a shorter commercial d) improving the animation quality
5. Play **Track 9.7**	a) He is working with this agency for the first time. b) He preferred the writers at the previous ad agency. c) He is head of the toothpaste company. d) He is unconcerned about the script changes.

Play **Track 9.8**	Listen to the third part of the conversation.
6. Play **Track 9.9**	a) disappointed b) angry c) excited d) pleased
7. Play **Track 9.10**	a) It requires more resources. b) It is on schedule. c) It is pending approval. d) It needs a new product.
8. Play **Track 9.11**	a) He has provided useful advice. b) She has enjoyed working with him. c) He has another project for her company. d) She has received payment for the ad.

Listening Part 2: Listening to a Daily Life Conversation

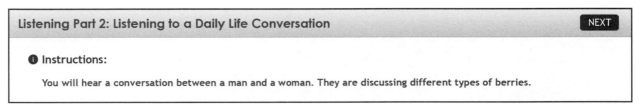

Listening Part 2: Listening to a Daily Life Conversation   **NEXT**

ℹ **Instructions:**

You will hear a conversation between a man and a woman. They are discussing different types of berries.

Play **Track 10.1**	Listen to the conversation.
1. Play **Track 10.2**	a) The woman offers assistance. b) The man requests information. c) The woman asks for directions. d) The man introduces himself.
2. Play **Track 10.3**	a) He will make it from blueberries. b) He will need a lot of berries. c) He will add a lot of sugar to it. d) He will make it with a little honey.
3. Play **Track 10.4**	a) to check if the berries they found are safe to eat b) to read some information about bees dying c) to see what a black raspberry looks like d) to find a list of foods that need bees to grow
4. Play **Track 10.5**	a) They are both allergic to bees. b) They are both grateful for bees. c) They are both afraid of bees. d) They are both optimistic about bees.

5. Play **Track 10.6**	a) their disappearance b) their ability to sting c) their habitat d) their daily routine

Listening Part 3: Listening for Information

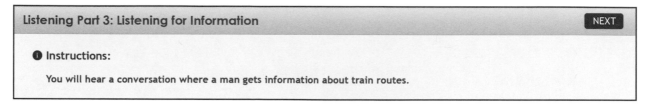

Listening Part 3: Listening for Information	NEXT
❶ Instructions:	
You will hear a conversation where a man gets information about train routes.	

Play **Track 11.1**	Listen to the conversation.
1. Play **Track 11.2**	a) The man is asking about current train specials. b) The man needs to book an urgent trip to Boston. c) The man wants information about train travel. d) The man is planning a family trip to Montreal.
2. Play **Track 11.3**	a) The cabin would be too crowded for the children. b) His children would dislike the meals offered. c) His children would be bored on the trip. d) The tickets would be too costly with the children.
3. Play **Track 11.4**	a) He is surprised by what the fare excludes. b) He is wondering if there is a deal. c) He is planning to purchase a ticket. d) He is curious about longer train trips.
4. Play **Track 11.5**	a) Boston b) Vancouver c) Toronto d) Montreal
5. Play **Track 11.6**	a) She makes no comment about the comparison. b) She argues that train service is more enjoyable. c) She describes the scenic delights of train travel. d) She recommends the shorter trip to Montreal.
6. Play **Track 11.7**	a) send a complaint about high ticket prices b) check the website for special rates to Montreal c) fly to Vancouver instead of taking the train d) purchase himself a round-trip ticket to Montreal

---

LEARNING FOCUS

- Understanding pauses, intonation, and stress
- Answering questions about general meaning
- Answering questions about specific details
- Following a sequence of events
- Note-taking
- Test practice

In Listening Part 4: Listening to a News Item, you will hear a report which focuses on an event that takes place in a Canadian community. You will be assessed on your ability to understand what the story is about. Some of the questions will test your general comprehension of the event; others will ask about specific details or require that you make inferences.

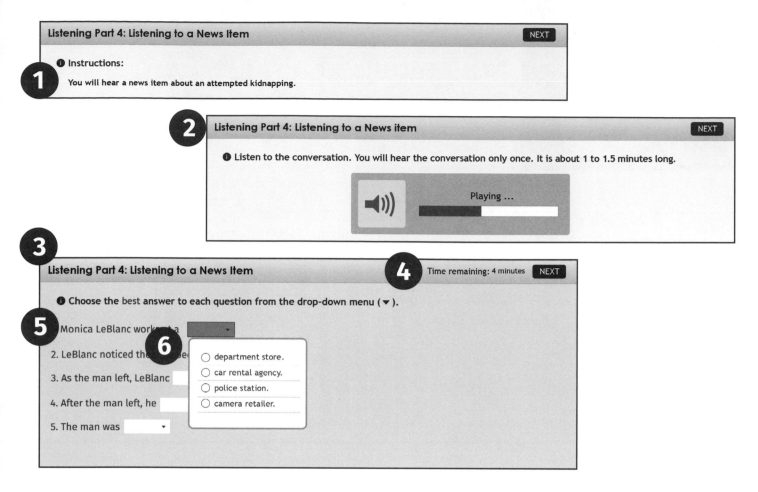

Listening Part 4: Listening to a News Item NEXT

1 ❶ Instructions:
You will hear a news item about an attempted kidnapping.

2 Listening Part 4: Listening to a News item NEXT

❶ Listen to the conversation. You will hear the conversation only once. It is about 1 to 1.5 minutes long.

Playing …

3 Listening Part 4: Listening to a News Item **4** Time remaining: 4 minutes NEXT

❶ Choose the best answer to each question from the drop-down menu (▼).

5 1. Monica LeBlanc works at a [▼]

6

2. LeBlanc noticed th...
- ○ department store.
- ○ car rental agency.
- ○ police station.
- ○ camera retailer.

3. As the man left, LeBlanc

4. After the man left, he

5. The man was [▼]

① The prelistening statement provides the context for the news item before the audio starts.

② Part 4 is a short news story delivered by one speaker.

③ Part 4 contains sentence-completion questions.

④ Be aware of the time remaining and be sure to answer all questions.

⑤ There are five questions in Part 4. The questions are given in text format, not audio.

⑥ Click on the box to see the options to complete each sentence. There will always be four choices.

Understanding Pauses, Intonation, and Stress

When you listen to audio with one speaker, such as the news report in Listening Part 4 in CELPIP, it is important to notice the small hints and signs that help you follow along. Three of these signs are pauses, intonation, and stressed words.

Pauses

Pauses are typically used for the following:

> Access the following audio via the Focus LS Resource Portal; the link is found in the Introduction.

TYPE OF PAUSE	EXAMPLE
Separating ideas from each other—pauses can separate individual ideas or groups of ideas	Play **Unit 3 – Track 1.1**. Sunset Beach is a popular tourist spot in Vancouver, [pause] but it can get overcrowded on holiday weekends.
Indicating extra information	Play **Unit 3 – Track 1.2**. The doctor's office is just a short bus ride from here, but [pause] if you want my opinion, [pause] you should just walk.
Emphasizing important words	Play **Unit 3 – Track 1.3**. Please pay attention to the following rule because it is [pause] very [pause] important.

Activity 1A

Listen to the audio and decide what kind of pause the highlighted phrases contain. These are shown in the transcript below. Circle your choice for each pause; the first has been done for you. Play **Unit 3 - Track 2.**

> An Ontario resident ordered some fast food **1. on Friday, but instead** of getting a bag of hot chicken, **2. he got a bag of cold hard cash. 3.** Richard Coleman, a third-year law student at the University of Toronto, pulled up to the drive-thru window of the popular Charlie's Chicken restaurant on Broadway and ordered a chicken burger and **4. french fries to go. At the first** stoplight on his way home, Coleman reached inside the take-out bag for his chicken burger and pulled out a **5. bundle of cash instead.** "I couldn't believe it!" said Coleman.

1. a) separate ideas *(circled)*	2. a) separate ideas
b) indicate extra information	b) indicate extra information
c) emphasize important words	c) emphasize important words

Continue →

3. a) separate ideas
    b) indicate extra information
    c) emphasize important words

4. a) separate ideas
    b) indicate extra information
    c) emphasize important words

5. a) separate ideas
    b) indicate extra information
    c) emphasize important words

Intonation

Intonation—the way the voice goes up and down—is also important when listening to English. It tells listeners more about the meaning of what the speaker is saying and how they feel about it. Note that intonation is used in a variety of ways in English speech, but that this unit will focus on the three most common patterns: falling, rising, and falling then rising.

Falling intonation describes how the voice falls at the end of a phrase or a sentence. This intonation is commonly used with WH questions.

Play **Unit 3 - Track 3.1**.

What is the time?

When will the movie start?

Falling intonation is also used to express statements of fact and certainty. Play **Unit 3 - Track 3.2**.

I like hockey.

Rising intonation describes how the voice rises at the end of a phrase or sentence. This intonation is commonly used with yes/no questions.

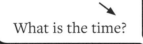

Play **Unit 3 - Track 3.3**.

The new boss starts today, doesn't he?

Are you a teacher?

Falling then rising intonation describes how the voice falls then rises at the end of a phrase or sentence. This type of intonation often tells the listener that what is being discussed might change, or there is more to be said about the topic.

Play **Unit 3 - Track 3.4**.

I don't have a camera quite yet.

Although the speaker does not have a camera now, it is clear that he is likely to get one in the future.

Falling then rising intonation can also be used with questions to make them sound more polite.

Play **Unit 3 - Track 3.5**.

> Would you like me to get you your bill now?

Activity 1B

Listen to the audio and draw a falling arrow (↘), rising arrow (↗), or falling then rising arrows (↘↗) in the blank to show the intonation on the last word or two of each sentence.
Play **Unit 3 – Track 4.1–4.6**.

1.	Excuse me, which way is the train station?	_____
2.	We have a meeting today, right?	_____
3.	Are you going to Sasha's graduation?	_____
4.	I think we should go that way.	_____
5.	Have you ever been to the theatre?	_____
6.	Have you seen the Celebration of Lights?	_____

Word Stress

Word stress is another hint that allows listeners to make sense of what is being said. Stressed words are often the most important words in a phrase or sentence. These keys words are often essential when listening for details.

Listen to **Unit 3 – Track 5** and read along with the text below; the stressed words are bolded.

> **Many tourists** assume that **Whistler** is only a **winter** destination. They are often **surprised** to learn that it provides many **summer** activities **as well**.

Note that in this passage, the words that the speaker emphasizes are helpful in gaining a general understanding of the main ideas.

Activity 1C

Listen to the audio and underline the stressed words in the excerpts below.
Play **Unit 3 - Track 6.1**.

> If we want to make it for the 4 o'clock ferry to Vancouver Island, we will need to arrive at the terminal before 3 o'clock. So, please try to be ready to leave by 2.

Play **Unit 3 - Track 6.2.**

> Last Friday, visitors to the Bridal Falls park received a welcome surprise. Actors in Victorian costumes presented a traditional travelling tea service. Guests were treated to fresh pastries, sandwiches, and three varieties of local tea.

After you checked your answers, did you notice anything about which words were stressed? As mentioned earlier, words are often stressed to highlight key information in someone's speech. Therefore, even if you don't understand or you didn't quite catch some words, listening for the stressed words should still give you a basic outline of what was discussed.

Answering Questions about General Meaning

In Unit 1, three types of questions that can be found in the Listening Test were introduced: general meaning, specific detail, and inference. In this unit, you will learn about general meaning and specific detail questions. Inference questions will be discussed in Unit 5.

General meaning questions assess your overall understanding of a conversation or report. To answer this type of question to the best of your ability, it is important to be able to separate the passage into two of its components: **topic** and **main ideas**.

Identifying the Topic

Being able to identify the topic of a conversation or report is extremely important. Sometimes it is obvious and clearly mentioned; other times, it is less clear and needs to be pieced together by listening to the entire passage.

One method of identifying the topic is to listen for repeated ideas. The more often certain words or their synonyms are used throughout a passage, the more likely they apply to the topic of the passage. These words are often called "key words." Key words can be almost any part of speech (noun, verb, adjective, adverb) but are most often nouns.

Activity 2

Listen to the audio and write down the key words and their variations which are repeated throughout the passage. The answers can be one or more words each—try to write down five or six. Then, compare your notes with the Answer Key. The first one has been done for you. Play **Unit 3 – Track 7.**

KEY WORDS		
Ontario resident		

Identifying Main Ideas

The difference between topics and main ideas is that the topic will appear throughout a passage, while a main idea will appear in a section. For example, in the following excerpt, the topic is finding a bag of money, and the three main ideas in this excerpt are related to Coleman's reaction, where the money came from, and why the money was given to him.

> [**Idea 1**] "I couldn't believe it!" said Coleman. "I immediately pulled over to the side of the road because I was afraid I'd get into an accident."

> [**Idea 2**] The money, which totalled over two thousand dollars, was the restaurant's deposit from the previous day. Ralph Black, the owner of Charlie's Chicken, had put the money in a paper take-out bag because he had run out of plastic bank deposit bags.

> [**Idea 3**] While he was on the phone, a drive-thru cashier unknowingly gave the bag to Coleman, thinking it was his take-out order.

Putting It All Together to Answer General Meaning Questions

Now that you understand how to identify topics and main ideas, you are ready to answer general meaning questions. General meaning questions are usually easy to recognize because they tend to use words like "overall," "mainly," and "mostly." They often ask what the passage is about or what the main problem is. The following examples show some typical general meaning questions:

> What is the problem?
> a) Someone has spilled tea on her coat.
> b) The attendant cannot find her coat.
> c) There are two identical winter coats.
> d) One ticket number goes with two coats.

> What does the man mainly talk about?
> a) which rooms should have a fan
> b) how ceiling fans keep a room warm
> c) what to consider when buying a fan
> d) why fans have remote controls

> When discussing bees, what do they talk about the most?
> a) their disappearance
> b) their ability to sting
> c) their habitat
> d) their daily routine

To better understand how to approach general meaning questions, consider the following steps used to answer a question about the passage introduced in Activity 2.

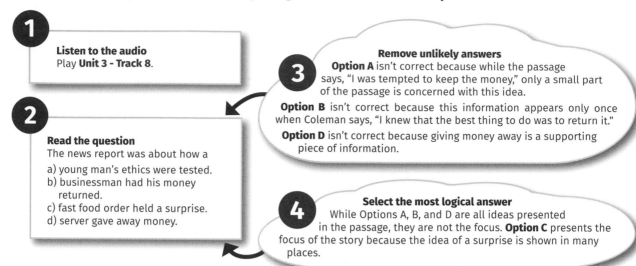

1 Listen to the audio
Play **Unit 3 - Track 8**.

2 Read the question
The news report was about how a
a) young man's ethics were tested.
b) businessman had his money returned.
c) fast food order held a surprise.
d) server gave away money.

3 Remove unlikely answers
Option A isn't correct because while the passage says, "I was tempted to keep the money," only a small part of the passage is concerned with this idea.
Option B isn't correct because this information appears only once when Coleman says, "I knew that the best thing to do was to return it."
Option D isn't correct because giving money away is a supporting piece of information.

4 Select the most logical answer
While Options A, B, and D are all ideas presented in the passage, they are not the focus. **Option C** presents the focus of the story because the idea of a surprise is shown in many places.

Below is an excerpt that demonstrates how the answer is found.

> An Ontario resident ordered some fast food on Friday, but instead of getting a bag of hot chicken, he got a bag of cold, hard cash . . .

The idea of a fast food order holding a surprise is introduced in this excerpt. A bag meant for chicken is found to contain money instead. This is, by nature, surprising.

> "I couldn't believe it!" said Coleman. "I immediately pulled over to the side of the road because I was afraid I'd get into an accident."

The idea of surprise is further expressed in the second excerpt. The passage goes into extensive detail to describe Coleman's reaction to this unexpected event, making **Option C** the best answer.

Answering Questions about Specific Details

Specific detail questions focus on the key pieces of information in a conversation or report. Specific details are used to support and develop main ideas. One of the main ideas in the example below is Richard Coleman's honesty ("Coleman is going to make a very honest lawyer."). While this statement can stand alone, it is also supported by details such as Coleman's statement, "I knew that the best thing to do was to return it."

> "I was tempted to keep the money," Coleman admitted, "but I knew that the best thing to do was to return it." Black told reporters, "I was quite surprised. I think most people would have kept the money—especially when you consider how expensive law school is! Coleman is going to make a very honest lawyer."

Putting It All Together to Answer Specific Detail Questions

Now that you understand how to identify specific details, you are ready to answer specific detail questions. One way to recognize that you are dealing with specific detail questions is that these questions usually ask what someone said or did. There may be other ways these questions appear, but they will always assess your ability to understand the key details from the passage. The following two examples show typical specific detail questions:

> Which coat did Jessica decide to buy?
> a) the red parka
> b) the yellow raincoat
> c) the blue trench coat
> d) the black peacoat

> What does the man say about neighbourhood associations?
> a) They help solve problems.
> b) They require too much time.
> c) They keep neighbourhoods safe.
> d) They improve people's relationships.

To better understand how to approach specific detail questions, consider the following the steps used to answer a question about the passage introduced in Activity 2.

1
Listen to the audio
Play **Unit 3 - Track 8**.

3 **Remove unlikely answers**
Option A isn't correct because the passage never talked about asking for a refund.
Option C isn't correct because the passage never mentioned Coleman refusing to eat at the restaurant.
Option D isn't correct because Coleman was already studying law at the beginning of the passage.

2
Read the question
Coleman decided to
a) demand a refund from the restaurant.
b) give back the cash to the owner.
c) stop eating at the restaurant.
d) start studying law at university.

4 **Select the most logical answer**
Option B presents the correct answer because the detail of giving back the cash to the owner was mentioned at one specific point in the passage.

"I was tempted to keep the money," Coleman admitted, "but I knew that the best thing to do was to return it." Black told reporters, "I was quite surprised. I think most people would have kept the money—especially when you consider how expensive law school is! Coleman is going to make a very honest lawyer."

The answer is found here since the passage says, "*I knew that the best thing to do was to return it* [the cash]."

35

It's important to note that, as is made clear by the example on the previous page, specific words from the listening passage are unlikely to appear in the answer options. Instead, the information may be paraphrased—meaning that ideas from the listening passage will be expressed using different words. The words in the correct answer option, "give back the cash to the owner," are not found in the passage. They are a paraphrase of ". . . but I knew the best thing was to return it."

Activity 3

Listen to the audio and answer the following questions. Indicate whether the question is about general meaning or specific details.
Play **Unit 3 - Track 9.**

1. General Meaning / Specific Detail

Mary Bryce was affected by
  a) false airline and hotel charges.
  b) hidden bank service fees.
  c) a scam targeting the elderly.
  d) bad advice from a workshop.

2. General Meaning / Specific Detail

The new workshop for seniors was designed to
  a) help seniors become more vigilant.
  b) educate banks on fraud protection.
  c) advise people on retirement planning.
  d) teach seniors how to invest money.

3. General Meaning / Specific Detail

Mary felt that the Canadian Bankers Association program
  a) needed better promotion.
  b) was incredibly beneficial.
  c) came too late to help her.
  d) should be free of charge.

4. General Meaning / Specific Detail

Mary's story raises awareness about
  a) affordable coupon programs.
  b) unfair bank service fees.
  c) dishonest phone marketing.
  d) financially struggling seniors.

Following a Sequence of Events

Unit 2 discussed how identifying pronoun usage can help you follow a sequence of events in a conversation. When you listen to news stories like those in Listening Part 4, you need to pay attention to words that describe *when* or *in what order* events happened. The first method is to listen for words describing dates or times. The second is to listen for sequencing words, some examples of which are in the table below.

SEQUENCING WORDS				
next	then	after that	finally	later
first	second	initially	in the beginning	meanwhile
at the same time	during	while	soon	until
before	after	just as	now	presently

Activity 4A

Listen to the passage and write down the words or phrases that describe when things happened.
Play **Unit 3 - Track 10.**

1. _____
   _____

2. _____
   _____

3. _____
   _____

4. _____
   _____

5. _____
   _____

6. _____
   _____

Activity 4B

Check your answers for Activity 4A and use them to help you complete the sentences below. Then listen to the audio and write the order of the sentences from 1 (the first sentence) to 5 (the last sentence) in the blanks in front of each sentence.
Play **Unit 3 - Track 10.**

____ a. Authorities are _____ trying to determine the motive for the crime.

____ b. _____,
      she noticed a man behaving erratically in one of the aisles.

____ c. _____, a security guard thwarted a kidnapping attempt by providing police with information that led to the rescue of a young girl.

____ d. _____, police put out an amber alert that a seven-year-old girl had been abducted

____ e. _____, police apprehended the man as he was speeding out of the city

Note-Taking

In Unit 2, a style of note-taking was introduced to help you when listening to two people having a conversation. In this unit, you will learn how to take notes on a news story delivered by a single speaker. This style of note-taking focuses on answering the following questions: Who? What? When? Where? Why?

To take notes using this style, take a sheet of paper and make a table with each question listed in a column on the left and space to answer the questions on the right. It is helpful to label who said what, so that you can remind yourself later.

WH WORD	NOTES
Who?	
What?	
When?	
Where?	
Why?	

Activity 5

Practice note-taking by listening to the audio and filling in the note template above.
Play **Unit 3 – Track 11**.

Test Practice

Using everything you have learned and the notes you have taken, listen to the audio and then choose the best answer to complete each sentence.

Play **Unit 3 – Track 11.**

Listening Part 4: Listening to a News Item NEXT

ⓘ Instructions:

You will hear a news item about a storm.

Play **Track 11**	Listen to the conversation.
1. The storm was a problem because	a) traffic was unusually heavy that day. b) the change in weather was unexpected. c) bad weather is uncommon in the area. d) the city had no salt for the roads.
2. Driving conditions were dangerous because	a) the roads required maintenance. b) salt trucks were blocking roads. c) it snowed many times in November. d) drivers were causing accidents.
3. Halifax motorist Alan Camcron	a) disliked the city's slow response. b) drives one of the salt trucks. c) had an accident on the highway. d) slipped on the black ice.
4. City official Samantha Park thinks that	a) commuters caused the problems. b) the city made a mistake. c) salt trucks need priority on roads. d) the city is doing its job correctly.
5. Listeners to the news would likely believe that	a) the salt trucks caused the traffic jams. b) the motorists were being careless. c) salt trucks will start earlier next time. d) city officials knew the storm was coming.

LEARNING FOCUS	• Recognizing visual cues
	• Recognizing verbal cues
	• Note-taking
	• Test Practice

In Listening Part 5: Listening to a Discussion, you will watch a video with three people who are discussing a topic. You will be assessed on your ability to follow the flow of a conversation among a small group of people and recall key details about the topic. As the conversation is presented in a video, you will be able to see the speakers and their surroundings, which can help you understand the situation.

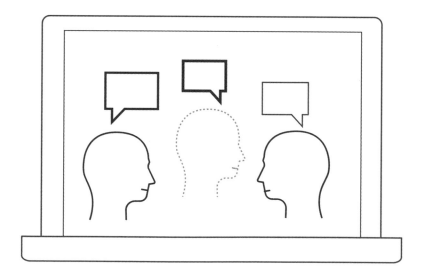

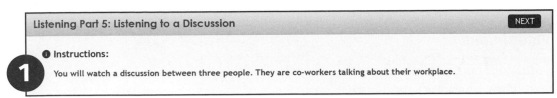

Listening Part 5: Listening to a Discussion — NEXT

ⓘ Instructions:

You will watch a discussion between three people. They are co-workers talking about their workplace.

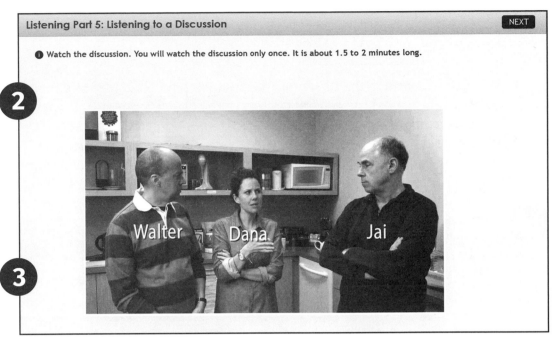

Listening Part 5: Listening to a Discussion — NEXT

ⓘ Watch the discussion. You will watch the discussion only once. It is about 1.5 to 2 minutes long.

Walter   Dana   Jai

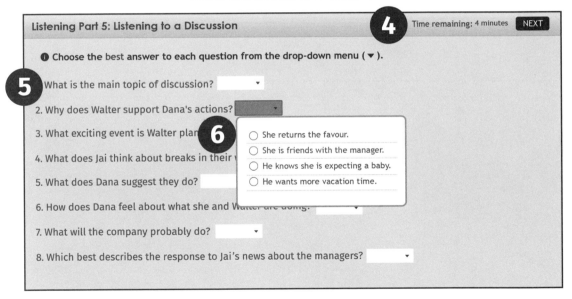

Listening Part 5: Listening to a Discussion — Time remaining: 4 minutes — NEXT

ⓘ Choose the best answer to each question from the drop-down menu (▼).

What is the main topic of discussion? ▼

2. Why does Walter support Dana's actions? ▼

3. What exciting event is Walter plan...

4. What does Jai think about breaks in their...

5. What does Dana suggest they do?

6. How does Dana feel about what she and Walter are doing?

7. What will the company probably do? ▼

8. Which best describes the response to Jai's news about the managers? ▼

○ She returns the favour.
○ She is friends with the manager.
○ He knows she is expecting a baby.
○ He wants more vacation time.

① The prelistening statement helps give the context before the video starts.

② Part 5 contains a video instead of an audio clip.

③ The discussion takes place between three people. First, you will see an image of the speakers in which each person is identified by name.

④ Be aware of the time remaining and be sure to answer all the questions.

⑤ There are eight questions in Part 5. The questions appear as text, not audio.

⑥ Click on the box to see the answer choices. There will always be four choices.

Recognizing Visual Cues

While watching the video, pay attention to visual cues that can help you understand the discussion. Some of these cues are found in the setting (where the speakers are), and some are found in the speakers' body language.

Setting

As in all parts of the Listening Test, there is a prelistening statement in Part 5 that will help you understand the general context of the listening passage. However, since the conversation in this part is presented in a video, you will be able to learn more about the situation by paying attention to visual details. Consider the setting of the conversation. Where are the speakers? Are they in a public place? Are they in a workplace? If so, what are the speakers' jobs? Paying attention to the setting will help you make sense of the conversation.

Activity 1

To practice identifying important visual aspects in a scene, imagine that you were presented with this image before the video began. Answer the following question to determine what information you can learn from it.

1. Where are the speakers?
    a) in an office
    b) in a coffee shop
    c) in a kitchen
    d) in a factory

Speakers

After you've used the setting to help you understand the situation, you need to be aware of how the speakers feel about the topic and what they are saying. The easiest way to do this is to pay attention to the speakers' body language: their facial expressions and posture. When you look at the speakers' body language, aim for a general understanding of their feelings: happy, sad, angry, confused, surprised, etc.

Activity 2

Look at the images below and answer the questions. Note that this activity is just meant to help you practice recognizing visual cues; you will not see image-based questions like this in the actual Listening Part 5.

Based on the pictures, how is each man/woman feeling at this moment?

1.

a) happy
b) sad
c) frustrated
d) amused

2.

a) excited
b) concerned
c) hopeful
d) bored

3.

a) joyful
b) confused
c) depressed
d) enthusiastic

Recognizing Verbal Cues

The other part of understanding a conversation in a video or in real life is being able to identify how people feel about a topic or each other from *what* they say and *how* they say it.

Formality

How formally people speak can give a lot of information about the relationship between the speakers and how well they know each other. Normally, we use informal English with our friends and family, and sometimes with co-workers. We become more formal as we talk to people with whom we are less familiar, and when we interact in more official settings (at a bank, in a court of law, etc.).

Informal		Level of Formality		Formal
• Friend • Family member	• Colleague • Acquaintance	• Stranger		• Supervisor • Police Officer

Tone of Voice

The tone of voice that someone uses can tell you about their mood. When someone speaks in a higher tone, it can mean that they are excited, uncertain, or surprised. If they use a lower tone, they might be certain or sad. Being able to identify a speaker's mood can help you understand the language they use.

> Access the audio via the Focus LS Resource Portal; the link is found in the Introduction.

Play **Unit 4 – Track 1.1–1.2** to hear examples of higher tones of voice.
Play **Unit 4 – Track 1.3–1.4** to hear examples of lower tones of voice.

Activity 3

Listen to each track and match it to the correct tone.
Play **Unit 4 – Track 2.1–2.5.**

1. Track 2.1 ___	a. depressed
2. Track 2.2 ___	b. inquiring
3. Track 2.3 ___	c. upset
4. Track 2.4 ___	d. uncertain
5. Track 2.5 ___	e. disbelieving

Word Choice

Word choice is another clue that helps listeners understand how someone feels about the topic being discussed. For example, if someone describes a conversation as a "dispute" or a "spat," they may be feeling negative or argumentative. Therefore, you should try to understand the emotional association of a word—and why the speaker chose to use *that specific word* instead of another—when listening to conversations.

Activity 4A

Read the words below and decide if they have a negative, neutral, or positive emotional meaning. Write each word under the correct heading.

Quarrel	Discussion	Debate	Sufficient	Moderate	Terrific	Boring
Acceptable	Terrible	Intriguing	Agreeable	Forgettable	Unreasonable	Memorable

Negative	Neutral	Positive

Activity 4B

Watch the video clips and decide what type of emotion the speakers are demonstrating during the discussion. Pay attention to each speaker's **tone**, as well as their language. What do their specific **word choices** say about their mood? Write "positive," "negative," or "neutral" next to each video.
Play **Unit 4 – Videos 1.1–1.5**.

Video 1.1	_____	Video 1.3	_____	Video 1.5	_____
Video 1.2	_____	Video 1.4	_____		

Note-Taking

Because Listening Part 5 is a conversation—like Parts 1, 2, and 3—it's easy to use the same note-taking style for this part. The only difference is that rather than having two columns (one for the man and one for the woman), there are three. Label the columns with the speakers' names, which will be displayed at the beginning of the video. See Unit 2 for more about taking notes on conversations.

Activity 5

Watch the video and write your notes in the space below.
Play **Unit 4 – Video 2.**

WH Word	ANGELA	JED	RONALDO
Who			
What			
When			
Where			
Why			

Test Practice

Using everything you have learned, watch the video and choose the best answer for each question.
Play **Unit 4 – Video 2.**

Listening Part 5: Listening to a Discussion   NEXT

🛈 **Instructions:**

You will watch a conversation among three employees, one woman and two men. They are discussing changes to a conference during a work break.

Play **Video 2**	Watch the discussion.
1. Why is the conference postponed?	a) The severe weather delayed travel plans. b) The space was given to another conference. c) Too few presenters expressed interest. d) Not enough bookings were made.
2. Why are the employees upset about the news?	a) The short notice is a huge inconvenience. b) They cannot attend the rescheduled conference. c) They wanted to take a holiday together. d) They were excited about the presentations.

3. Why does Angela have more information than the others?	a) She already received an email notice. b) She received a call from the hotel about it. c) She makes the staff travel arrangements. d) She overheard the director talking about it.
4. What is Ronaldo worried about?	a) attending the most interesting workshops b) getting a full refund from the hotel c) having enough time to change his schedule d) running out of time for his workshop
5. What does Ronaldo say about the conference?	a) The workshops should be more interesting. b) The presentations are groundbreaking. c) The conference is important for their careers. d) The company should pay for everything.
6. Why does Angela think the company will rebook everything?	a) It gets a discount with group reservations. b) It knows the new time and location. c) It paid these expenses for employees. d) It prefers everyone to travel together.
7. Which sentence best describes Angela?	a) She enjoys going to conferences. b) She is the company director. c) She likes to fix problems. d) She likes to share rumours.
8. What will likely happen next?	a) No one will be required to attend the conference. b) The company will plan a new conference. c) Staff will be reimbursed for expenses. d) Staff will be updated about the situation.

LEARNING FOCUS

- Recognizing reported speech
- Identifying facts and opinions
- Recognizing inference questions
- Note-taking
- Test practice

Listening Part 6: Listening for Viewpoints features a report in which you will hear multiple opinions about an issue. It tests your ability to combine information from different parts of the Listening passage, identify opinions, differentiate between opinions and facts, and make inferences. To answer the multiple-choice questions, you will need to understand differing views held by experts.

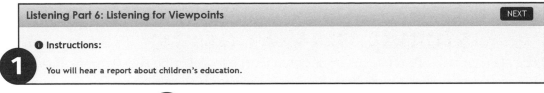

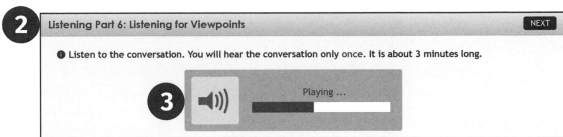

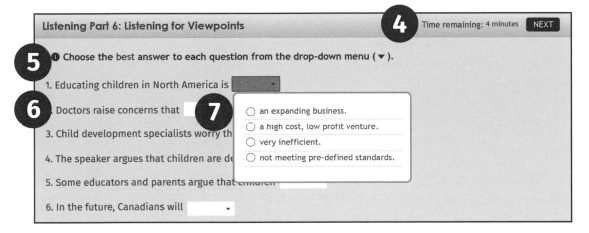

① The prelistening statement helps give the context before the audio starts.

② Part 6 is a report by a single speaker.

③ As you listen, try to identify the different viewpoints that are mentioned.

④ Be aware of the time remaining and be sure to answer all the questions.

⑤ Part 6 contains sentence-completion questions.

⑥ There are six questions in Part 6. The questions appear as text, not audio.

⑦ Click on the box to see the answer choices. There will always be four choices.

Recognizing Reported Speech

Since the speaker is talking about other people's opinions, the speaker may not use their exact words. Instead, the speaker will often use his or her own words to describe these viewpoints. The speaker may use a phrase like, "The police chief declared that he was opposed to the new parking regulations." We don't know the police chief's exact words; we only hear the speaker's *reported speech* describing what the police chief said.

The speaker in Listening Part 6 will report speech from a variety of sources. To keep track of these various sources, it is useful to note the names, job titles, or other descriptors of people mentioned in the passage. However, it can also be useful to pay attention to words used to report speech, as these will help you understand the general meaning of a person's statement. Phrases like "Davis questioned . . ." or "Patel counters . . ." suggest disagreement. A phrase like "Zhang believes . . ." tells you that what comes next will be an opinion rather than a statement of fact. In this next activity, you will learn about other words related to reported speech that can help you better understand the various viewpoints expressed in Listening Part 6.

Activity 1

Listen to the audio, and write the missing reported speech verb in the blanks.

> Play **Unit 5 - Track 1.**
> Access audio via the Focus LS Resource Portal; the link is found in the Introduction.

---

1. Chief of Police Andrew Smith _____ that the maximum penalty of $5,000 does little to deter.

2. He _____ not only for increased fines but also for time in prison.

3. However, legal philosopher Susan Bennett _____ that foreseeable consequences are not the only motivating factor.

4. She _____ that many people consider illegal downloading to be a victimless crime.

5. Bennett _____ about another common justification that illegal downloading provides free promotion for the aforementioned artists.

6. But as lawyer Ethan Miller _____, these companies were built on the backs of internet pirates.

Identifying Facts and Opinions

In Listening for Viewpoints, you will need to identify key facts, understand the experts' opinions, and demonstrate that you can recognize the difference between facts and opinions. One useful strategy is to watch out for key indicator words that introduce a statement that is either a fact or opinion. Some words that indicate that a statement is a fact are "report," "state," and "say." Some words that indicate that a statement is an opinion are "believe," "argue," and "consider."

Activity 2

Listen to the following tracks, and identify whether each statement is a fact or an opinion. Write "fact" or "opinion" in each blank.

1. **Unit 5 - Track 2.1** _____   5. **Unit 5 - Track 2.5** _____

2. **Unit 5 - Track 2.2** _____   6. **Unit 5 - Track 2.6** _____

3. **Unit 5 - Track 2.3** _____   7. **Unit 5 - Track 2.7** _____

4. **Unit 5 - Track 2.4** _____   8. **Unit 5 - Track 2.8** _____

Activity 3

Listen to the audio and answer the questions. Pay special attention to word choice as a way to help identify viewpoints.
Play **Unit 5– Track 1.**

1. Which statement best summarizes Susan Bennett's opinion?
   a) Bennett disagrees that limited punishments are the sole reason for internet piracy.
   b) Bennett also believes that punishments help stop internet piracy.
   c) Bennett thinks that adding a prison sentence to current fines will scare people away from piracy.
   d) Bennett argues that internet piracy is okay because it provides free advertising.

2. Which statement best summarizes Ethan Miller's perspective?
   a) Miller suggests that streaming companies were founded by criminals.
   b) Miller states that authorized streaming companies and internet pirates have the same source.
   c) Miller believes that most Canadians are aware that asking a friend to send them a song means breaking the law.
   d) Miller argues that using streaming services does not reduce the legal risks its users face.

Recognizing Inference Questions

On the Listening Test, the answers to some questions may not be explicitly mentioned in the conversation or monologue. Instead, you will have to put pieces of information from the passage together, and make logical connections to find the answer. To better understand how to approach this type of question, known as inference questions, consider the following the steps used to answer a question about the passage related to internet piracy.

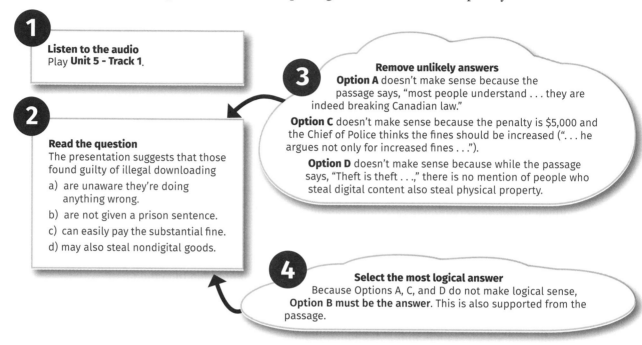

1
Listen to the audio
Play **Unit 5 - Track 1**.

2
Read the question
The presentation suggests that those found guilty of illegal downloading

a) are unaware they're doing anything wrong.
b) are not given a prison sentence.
c) can easily pay the substantial fine.
d) may also steal nondigital goods.

3
Remove unlikely answers
Option A doesn't make sense because the passage says, "most people understand . . . they are indeed breaking Canadian law."
Option C doesn't make sense because the penalty is $5,000 and the Chief of Police thinks the fines should be increased (". . . he argues not only for increased fines . . .").
Option D doesn't make sense because while the passage says, "Theft is theft . . .," there is no mention of people who steal digital content also steal physical property.

4
Select the most logical answer
Because Options A, C, and D do not make logical sense, **Option B must be the answer**. This is also supported from the passage.

Below is an excerpt that demonstrates how the answer is found.

Given Canada's reputation as a reasonably law-abiding society, one has to ask: why do so many people knowingly break internet law? Chief of Police Andrew Smith claims that the maximum penalty of $5,000 does little to deter, and he argues not only for increased fines but also for time in prison. Theft is theft, he says.

The answer to the question is found here. Because the worst penalty is a fine, time in prison must not be a current punishment.

The answer is also supported by this phrase since it supports the idea that currently there is no prison time.

Activity 4

Listen to the audio and complete the following sentences. In these questions, the answer will not be explicitly stated—you will need to use the information presented in the audio passage and make logical connections.
Play **Unit 5 – Track 3**.

1. Vince Levin probably supports
   a) fixed pricing for Canadian dairy products.
   b) high interest rates on loans to new farmers.
   c) tougher fines by federal food inspection agencies.
   d) marketing training for new farmers starting up.

2. The people most likely to agree with Rebecca Hogue are
   a) large companies producing pesticides for farmers.
   b) specialty crop farmers on family-run farms.
   c) international farmers exporting products to Canada.
   d) financially struggling restaurant owners.

Note-Taking

In Units 2 and 3, two variations on note organization were introduced. This unit will introduce a third variation that is best suited to Listening Part 6: viewpoint-focused organization. This style focuses on arranging information around the different individuals or organizations that are mentioned in the report. To create this layout, take a sheet of paper and create a table with at least three columns. Below that, write "Topic."

NOTES		
VIEWPOINT 1	**VIEWPOINT 2**	**VIEWPOINT 3**
TOPIC:		

As you listen to the audio, use each column to gather information about a different person or organization. Remember, you do not need to write full ideas. Instead, write key words and phrases. If you want, you can use the shorthand and symbols mentioned in Unit 2.

Activity 5

Practice note-taking by listening to the audio and completing the chart on the previous page. Play **Unit 5 – Track 4**.

Test Practice

Using everything you have learned, and the notes you have made, choose the best answer to complete each sentence.
Play **Unit 5 – Track 4**.

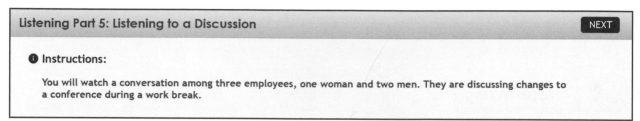

| Listening Part 5: Listening to a Discussion | NEXT |

ⓘ Instructions:

You will watch a conversation among three employees, one woman and two men. They are discussing changes to a conference during a work break.

Play **Unit 5 – Track 4**	Listen to the conversation.
1. The presentation mainly focuses on the	a) differences in how a professor's time is used now and in the past. b) contrasts between learning in the pre-digital and digital age. c) advantages of online learning for today's university students. d) benefits of traditional learning materials in the digital classroom.
2. The use of computer technology in education	a) has changed over time. b) is a very recent development. c) is the reason for digitizing books. d) has not always been supported.
3. Professor Diamonti seems to	a) welcome educational technology. b) be hesitant toward new technology. c) prefer traditional teaching methods. d) see pros and cons to digitization.
4. Educational psychologists would likely agree that today's students	a) have better health overall than students in previous generations. b) lack the organizational skills to manage their course loads. c) spend more time with their friends than in previous generations. d) have increased difficulty retaining what was learned in class.
5. The speaker suggests that technology at the university has	a) created problems for his staff. b) made the students lazier about research. c) been an asset to his department. d) caused professors to publish less research.
6. The speaker would most likely agree that	a) libraries are no longer considered places of quiet study. b) print books are being replaced by more versatile resources. c) projection screens are valuable only to certain disciplines. d) videoconferencing capabilities are most useful to administrators.

UNIT 6

Overview of the Speaking Test

LEARNING FOCUS

- Format of the Speaking Test
- Scoring
- Test-taking strategies for Speaking
- Improving your speaking

The Speaking Test measures your ability to communicate in day-to-day situations. It is made up of eight tasks, each of which requires you to speak in a common context, such as giving advice, expressing your opinion, and talking about personal experiences. Some of these tasks include images which are used to test a variety of skills, including describing situations, and making predictions and comparisons.

The Speaking Test is entirely computer delivered. You will read instructions on the screen and speak into the microphone of your headset. Your responses will be recorded by the computer and then sent to a team of human raters for assessment.

In this unit, you will become familiar with the overall format of the Speaking Test. You will also learn about the four categories of performance standards used by CELPIP Raters to assess your speaking.

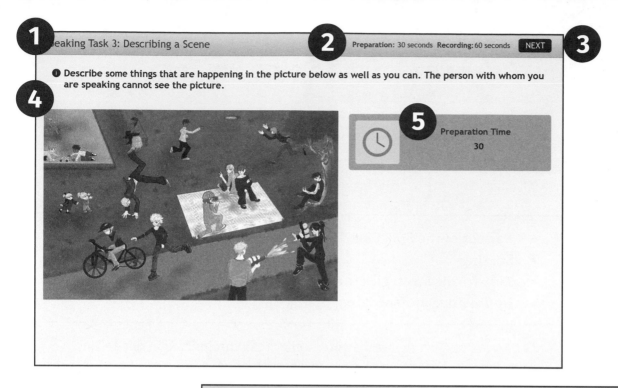

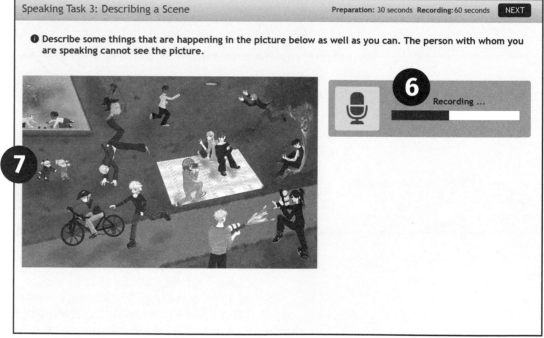

① The title reminds you where you are in the test.

② The Preparation and Recording Times vary for each task.

③ Use the NEXT button to move to the next part before the timer reaches zero. You cannot move back.

④ The task instructions will appear at the top of the page.

⑤ Use the Preparation Time to plan your response—do not speak yet.

⑥ Speak during the Recording Time. The progress bar indicates how much time is left.

⑦ Images appear in Tasks 3, 4, 5, and 8 only.

Format of the Speaking Test

There are eight tasks in the Speaking Test, as well as an unscored practice task at the beginning. You will have about 20 minutes to complete the Speaking Test.

SPEAKING TASK	DESCRIPTION
Practice Task	You will be asked a question in order to check that the mic is working correctly and to see how the timers work. Simply answer the question to get used to the mic set-up. If there is a problem, ask an invigilator for help.
Giving Advice	Help someone to either make a decision or prepare for something.
Talking about a Personal Experience	Tell a story about an event from your past.
Describing a Scene	Describe an image to someone who cannot see it.
Making Predictions	Talk about what will happen next in the same image.
Comparing and Persuading	Choose between two things and persuade someone to agree with your choice.
Dealing with a Difficult Situation	Choose between two solutions to a problem and explain your choice to a friend, family member, or member of the community.
Expressing Opinions	Express your opinion about a common issue in Canadian society.
Describing an Unusual Situation	Describe an image of an unusual object or situation to someone who cannot see the image.
TOTAL TIME	**About 20 minutes**

Tip

- Read **all** instructions to the right of the "instructions" symbol ❶ very carefully.
- Do your best to speak for the full duration of your Recording Time.
- Even if you are nervous, try not to speak too quickly—it can make your response difficult to understand.
- Avoid lengthy pauses.

Scoring

CELPIP Raters assess your Speaking responses using these four performance standards:

Content/Coherence: Quality of ideas and how well they flow together
Vocabulary: Selection and use of vocabulary, phrases, and idioms
Listenability: Understandability and fluency of your response
Task Fulfillment: Completion of all task requirements

The list below identifies the key features of each of these performance standards that contribute to a high-scoring response.

Content/Coherence

- Ideas are strong and relevant.
- Ideas are clear, well organized, and easy to follow.
- Ideas have been combined effectively, with supporting details, to form a meaningful and coherent response.

Vocabulary

- Vocabulary demonstrates a range of suitable words and phrases.
- Words and phrases have been combined effectively to express precise meaning.
- Selected words and phrases support easy understanding.

Listenability

- Response includes appropriate rhythm, pronunciation, and intonation.
- Response contains a variety of sentence types.
- Response demonstrates good control of grammar, pauses, interjections, and self-correction.

Task Fulfillment

- Response addresses all parts of the task and follows the given instructions.
- Tone is appropriate for the situation.
- Overall purpose of the task has been achieved within the time limit.

Test-Taking Strategies for Speaking

Using the Preparation Time

Use the Preparation Time to read the instructions and consider what you will speak about. Ensure that you fully understand these instructions, as this will make it easier to respond thoroughly and accurately during the Recording Time. Be ready to speak as soon as the Recording Time begins, and note that these times vary from task to task. The Preparation Time may seem relatively short, but keep in mind that if somebody asks you a question in everyday life, you won't have time to tell that person to wait while you plan an answer. Instead, you would try to quickly respond. Thus, the CELPIP Test reflects your ability to use English naturally in everyday contexts.

Brainstorming Ideas

In case you have difficulty thinking of something to say during your Preparation Time, you can use the notepaper provided to you during the official test. It may be helpful to brainstorm (write rough notes about) some ideas. Start off by writing any ideas that seem connected to the topic. The act of writing down a few words—any words—can help reduce anxiety and focus your mind on the task. Once you have something down on paper, select your best ideas and decide on the order in which you will speak about them. If you can come up with two or three main ideas during the Preparation Time, you can focus on developing these ideas with supporting details during the Recording Time.

Self-Correction

During the Speaking Test, if you make a small mistake when speaking, it's okay to correct yourself and move on. Try to do this quickly; don't waste time explaining your self-correction. For example, don't say, "Oh sorry, I didn't mean that. I mean . . ."

Avoiding Repetition

As much as possible, you should try to show the range of your English. Instead of repeating the same words or phrases, do your best to find new ways to express yourself. That way, you will show the raters the full extent of your vocabulary.

Volume and Speed

It's best to speak at a normal volume, with the microphone close to your lips but not touching them. There is no need to raise your voice, nor to whisper.

Try to use natural rhythm, pacing, and intonation. If you speak too quickly, it may be difficult for raters to understand you. If you speak too slowly, long pauses between words may also make it difficult to understand the flow of your response.

Tone

The word "tone" refers to the emotion expressed when speaking, both in terms of the sound of your voice and the words you choose to express yourself. Ensure that your tone is appropriate to the situation in each task.

Providing a Complete Response

There are often multiple instructions in each Speaking task. As you are speaking, make sure to complete all these instructions and speak for the full time. Don't worry too much if you get cut off at the end—just focus on developing all your main ideas in the time that's allotted to you.

Staying on Topic

Everything you say in your response should be related to the instructions of the Speaking task. Talking about unrelated ideas could lower your score. If parts of your response are off topic, it can become difficult for the raters to follow your ideas. It can also suggest that you do not fully understand the instructions. You only have between 60 and 90 seconds to speak for each task, so do your best to make everything you say count toward fully developing your response.

Improving Your Speaking

In preparing for the Speaking Test, there are various ways to improve your skills. Practice speaking English as often as you can, whether it's conversations with friends, family, or co-workers; or even with acquaintances in clubs and hobby groups. You may want to regularly record yourself as you study for the test, and play your responses back to find areas in which you could improve. In addition, you may wish to keep a daily journal of new English words and phrases that you've learned. Review these terms frequently and try to use them while speaking whenever you can; this will help increase your range of vocabulary.

UNIT 7

Giving Advice

LEARNING FOCUS	• Using "advise" versus "advice" • Giving advice • Identifying common errors • Self-assessment • Rate the response

In Speaking Task 1: Giving Advice, you will give advice to a person about a common situation or event. Read the instructions thoroughly to make sure that you understand the situation. You should consider who you are talking to and try to come up with at least a few different pieces of advice that would help him or her. You should also support your advice with reasons and examples. Remember to *directly* address the listener in this task. For example, if you needed to advise your friend Molly about preparing for French class, you might say, "Hi Molly. So I hear you're unsure about how to get ready for class. I would suggest that . . ." You would *not* say, "I would suggest that Molly . . ."

...aybe you should. Ha...
...ld suggest. You could try. You coul...
. to. Have you thought about. Maybe you sho...
...ed, I advise you to. I would suggest. You could try.
...ys. Well, you might want to. Have you thought about.
...u should. Have you considered, I advise you to. I would
...'ou could try. You could always. Well, you might want
...u thought about. Maybe you should. Have you conside...
...o. I would suggest. You could try. You could always
...+ to. Have you thought about. Maybe you sho...
...dvise you to. I would suggest. You co...
...ight want to. Have you t...
...onsi...
...ould

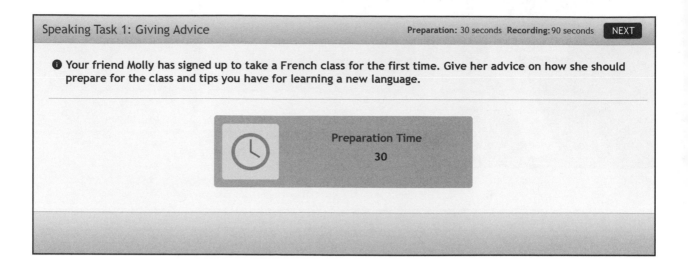

Speaking Task 1: Giving Advice   Preparation: 30 seconds Recording: 90 seconds   NEXT

ⓘ Your friend Molly has signed up to take a French class for the first time. Give her advice on how she should prepare for the class and tips you have for learning a new language.

Preparation Time
30

Using "Advise" Versus "Advice"

Test takers sometimes get confused about how to correctly use the words "advise" (əd'vʌɪz) and "advice" (əd'vʌɪs). Here are some pointers:

- "Advise" is a verb. If directly advising someone about what action to take, you could say, "I advise you to . . . (*do something*)."
- "Advice" is an uncountable noun. You cannot add "s" to the end of "advice."
- You might make statements like, "My advice is . . ." or "If I can give you some advice . . ."
- If you want to use "advice" in a countable form, you will have to add the phrase "piece of," as in "I can give you a piece of advice . . ." or "Let me give you three pieces of advice . . ."

Activity 1

The following sentences are in response to the task at the top of the page. However, they contain errors related to the use of "advise" and "advice." Rewrite the sentences using the correct forms of these words.

1. I advice you to review all the new words you learn each day.

   _____

2. I think you should take my advices about speaking French as much as you can outside of class.

   _____

3. Listen carefully: I have an important advise for you.

   _____

4. My friends gave me a lot of advises when I first started learning a new language.

   _____

Continue ⌐→

5. I have a friend who gave me some advices that I didn't find useful, so I advice you to study for this class in whatever way works for you!

Giving Advice

There are several different ways of giving advice. Here are five patterns that you could use on the Speaking Test. These patterns sometimes include modals, which are verbs used to describe ability, possibility, permission, or obligation—for example, "could," "would," "should," "must," and "can." Modals are always used in conjunction with another verb. Note that these patterns are general concepts, and specific examples may vary slightly in word use.

Pattern 1: Subject + Modal + "not" (optional) + Base Verb + Object

This pattern is the simplest and most common. It is important that you do not say "to" before the verb.

- You should call your friend when you get home.
- You could try going to the play tonight.
- You must ask for permission.

Pattern 2: Subject + "might/may want to" + Base Verb + Object

This has the same function as Pattern 1 but is more polite.

- You may want to ask if that's okay.
- You might want to check with your boss to see if you can do that.

Pattern 3: Subject + "had better" + "not" (optional) + Base Verb + Object

This is more forceful than Patterns 1 and 2. It should not be used when speaking to people in positions of authority—for example, your boss or teacher.

- She had better talk to her parents first.
- You had better not take that job; it's too far away.

Pattern 4: "Why not" + Base Verb + Object?

Because this is phrased as a question, it is more polite than Pattern 3. However, since there is no obvious subject, you can only use it when giving advice directly to a person. For example, you can say, "Hi Debbie. Why not see if your sister is available to hang out this weekend?"

- Why not ask your teacher if you can hand in the assignment after the next class?
- Why not try the food first and then decide if you like it or not?

Pattern 5: "Why don't/doesn't" + Subject + Base Verb + Object?

This is different than Pattern 4 because it *does* include a subject. When you use this, make sure you choose the right form of "don't/doesn't" for your subject.

- Why doesn't your cousin ask her neighbour for help?
- Why doesn't he tell his boss what happened?

Activity 2

Read the context of each situation below and write **one** sentence with the given pattern. Then, try saying the sentence out loud. Edit any awkward phrasing that you notice, and try saying it once more.

1. Suggest to your co-worker that they should try to avoid being late after their lunch break.

   Why don't _____

   _____ (Pattern 5)

2. A friend has told you that they want to spend less money on groceries each month. Suggest some ways for them to reduce how much they spend.

   You had better _____

   _____ (Pattern 3)

3. Suggest to your manager that the company could use more computer-related training for workers using the internet.

   You might want to _____

   _____ (Pattern 2)

4. Suggest to your cousin, who is shy around strangers, that she should come out to meet new people more often.

   Why not _____

   _____ (Pattern 4)

5. Explain to a friend how to meet people and make friends when moving to a new place.

   You _____

   _____ (Pattern 1)

Continue ↳→

6. Your cousin is about to go to an important job interview dressed casually and without knowing much about that company. Give advice on what to do.

   You had better _____

   _____(Pattern 3)

7. A friend is taking a class in a foreign language but has had difficulty making any progress in the first 2 weeks. Suggest how she can deal with this issue.

   You _____

   _____(Pattern 1)

8. Your co-worker has designed a product logo that you know the managers don't approve of. Suggest how to change the logo.

   Why don't _____

   _____(Pattern 5)

Identifying Common Errors

The following are common errors that you should try to avoid when speaking. Avoiding these problems will make it easier for others to understand you and will help you perform at your best on the Speaking Test.

1. **Being Repetitive**

   Constantly repeating the same words in your response can suggest a lack of vocabulary. Try to draw on the full range of your vocabulary and show the raters how much you know.

2. **Confusing "Advice" with "Advise"**

   As mentioned at the beginning of this unit, some test takers confuse "advice" with "advise." Remember, "advice" is a noun ("Let me give you some **advice**.") and "advise" is a verb ("He **advised** me to bring an umbrella."). Do your best to avoid mixing up these similar-sounding words.

3. **Misusing Collocations**

   A collocation is a group of words that are commonly used together, such as "doing the dishes" or "making the bed." It would be incorrect to say "making the dishes" or "doing the bed." Collocations can be challenging because even a small mistake can result in a very different meaning. Therefore, make sure that you use these correctly in your response.

Activity 3

In the space provided below, identify examples of the three types of errors discussed in this section. This response may contain other types of errors, but for this activity, *only* focus on these three types of errors.

> Play **Unit 7 - Track 1**.
> Access the audio via the Focus LS Resource Portal; the link is found in the Introduction.

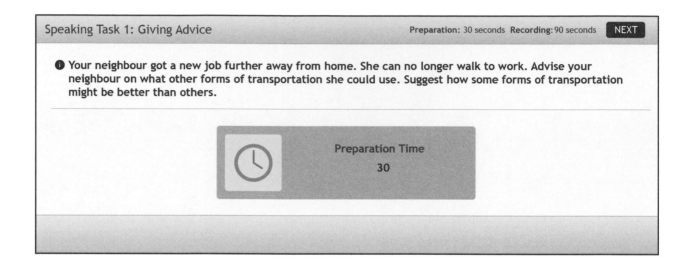

Speaking Task 1: Giving Advice Preparation: 30 seconds Recording: 90 seconds NEXT

ⓘ Your neighbour got a new job further away from home. She can no longer walk to work. Advise your neighbour on what other forms of transportation she could use. Suggest how some forms of transportation might be better than others.

Preparation Time
30

Hello, I heard you got a new job. So I suggest that-that . . . you just take a bus from the bus stop, near to our house. You can just buy a card that . . . um-reloadable. It will cost you a little, but it-it will be faster than having a cab. And you can also use MRT, it's also the same card that you will use for . . . for the bus, it can—and it will also be reloadable. From the bus stop, you just take the bus 305 and it will take around 15 to 20 minutes to your work. If in case you are not unsure, there will be a centre there that you can ask, or there will be a representative that can answer your question. But I am familiar with the job that you are going to transfer with, so I . . . I'll advice you to just take bus from house to work. So you can just reload your card from the MRT stations nearby and you can just ask the staff there to help you and guide you how to do. The earliest time of arrival of the bus will be 7 a.m., so I advise that you should be 15 minutes earlier prior to your departure.

1.	Being Repetitive

Continue ⌐→

2. Confusing "Advice" with "Advise"

3. Misusing Collocations

Self-Assessment

The "Self-Assessment" section gives you the opportunity to answer a practice question and record your response. You will then play back your response and use the CELPIP Speaking Checklist to identify the strengths and weaknesses of your response. A self-assessment section and checklist is included in each Speaking unit.

When you are checking your work, try to think like a CELPIP Rater. Remember the Performance Standards in Unit 6, and look for problems in those areas. Select (✓) "Yes" on the checklist if you think you have done something well, "Sometimes" if you have partially achieved a requirement, and "No" if you have missed a requirement.

Use a device (phone, laptop, etc.) to record your response to the following task and then play it back. Fill out the checklist as you listen. To practice timed responses for Speaking Task 1: Giving Advice, give yourself **30 seconds** to prepare and **90 seconds** to speak.

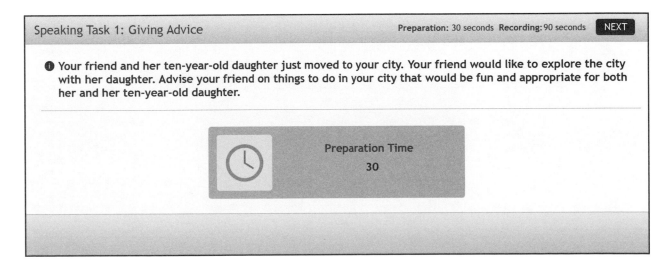

CELPIP SPEAKING CHECKLIST

	Yes	Sometimes	No
1. Did you address the listener directly?			
2. Did you speak clearly with minimal pauses and hesitations?			
3. Did you use appropriate rhythm, pronunciation, and intonation?			
4. Did you accurately use a variety of words?			
5. Did you avoid repeating ideas?			
6. Was your tone appropriate for the social context?			
7. Did you provide several different pieces of advice?			
8. Was your response clearly organized?			
9. Was your response long enough?			
10. Did you fully address the task?			

Rate the Response

The following are sample responses to the task from the Self-Assessment activity.

1. Play each response and circle the appropriate CELPIP Level range from the given choices.
2. Write down some of the strengths and weaknesses of each response.
   - You may wish to refer to the Performance Standards in Unit 6 to help you.
3. Check the Answer Key for an explanation of each response's level range.

Play **Unit 7 – Track 2.1**.

LEVEL M	LEVELS 3–4	LEVELS 5–6
Strengths:		
Weaknesses:		

Play **Unit 7 – Track 2.2**.

LEVELS 7–8	LEVELS 9–10	LEVELS 11–12
Strengths:		
Weaknesses:		

Play **Unit 7 – Track 2.3**.

LEVELS 7–8	LEVELS 9–10	LEVELS 11–12
Strengths:		
Weaknesses:		

LEARNING FOCUS

- Organizing your ideas
- Adding details to your response
- Using time sequencers
- Identifying common errors
- Self-assessment
- Rate the response

In Speaking Task 2: Talking about a Personal Experience, you will be asked to describe an experience from your life. It is perfectly acceptable to make up some of the details, if you like. You should choose a single experience and try to provide as many descriptive details as possible. As you will be talking about past events, be sure to use the past tense and include words and phrases that will help the listener keep track of the order of events.

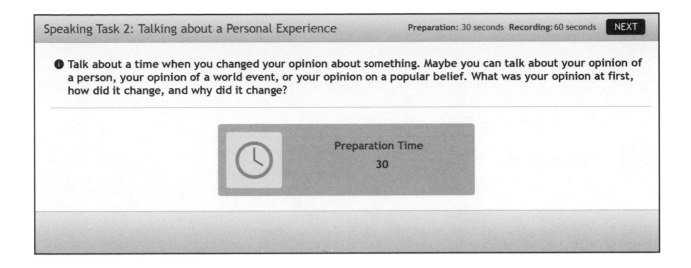

Speaking Task 2: Talking about a Personal Experience   Preparation: 30 seconds Recording: 60 seconds   NEXT

❶ Talk about a time when you changed your opinion about something. Maybe you can talk about your opinion of a person, your opinion of a world event, or your opinion on a popular belief. What was your opinion at first, how did it change, and why did it change?

Preparation Time
30

Organizing Your Ideas

The Speaking Task 2 instructions include around three questions, and you can use these questions to inform the main ideas of your response. Doing so will ensure that you completely fulfil the tasks outlined in the instructions.

Writing a brief outline—as in the following activities—can help with this, but keep in mind that you are *not required* to write anything during your Preparation Time. This is just a suggestion that may help with your brainstorming.

Activity 1A

Read the task at the top of this page. Then listen to the audio and pay attention to how this test taker's response was structured. Make notes of their organization using the outline below. The first one has been done for you.

Play **Unit 8 - Track 1.**
Access the audio via the Focus LS Resource Portal; the link is found in the Introduction.

Overview of the situation: *changed opinion of a colleague*

    What was the
    speaker's opinion?

    How did it change?

    Why did it change?

Conclusion/Resolution:

Adding Details to Your Response

Once you have your main points, it is important to consider how to develop these ideas using details and examples. Adding depth to each point can make the reasoning and explanations in your response easier to follow, and it further allows you to demonstrate your ability to use descriptive language.

Activity 1B

Listen again to **Unit 8 - Track 1** and, this time, note down the details the test taker used to support each main point. The first one has been done for you.

Overview of the situation:	*colleague helped teach speaker at new job*
What was the speaker's opinion?	
How did it change?	
Why did it change?	
Conclusion/Resolution:	

Activity 2A

Now you will have a chance to practice organizing your own response. Read the following task and fill in the chart. Make sure to write in point form; even a single word may be sufficient in some cases. Keep in mind that on the official test, you will have 30 seconds of Preparation Time for Task 2.

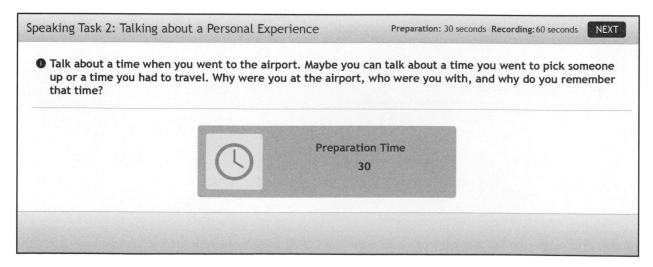

Speaking Task 2: Talking about a Personal Experience   Preparation: 30 seconds Recording: 60 seconds   NEXT

ⓘ **Talk about a time when you went to the airport. Maybe you can talk about a time you went to pick someone up or a time you had to travel. Why were you at the airport, who were you with, and why do you remember that time?**

Preparation Time
30

ORGANIZING YOUR IDEAS
Overview of the situation
Why were you at the airport?
Who were you with?
Why do you remember that time?
Conclusion/Resolution

Activity 2B

Now use a device to record your own response, using the notes you just made. Speak for 60 seconds. Play back your response and check that you answered each point of the question and added some details for each point.

For comparison, play **Unit 8 - Track 2**, which is a high-level response to this task.

Using Time Sequencers

Within your response, time sequencers can be a useful way of showing the progression of your story. Once you begin speaking, consider ways in which you can use time sequencers to make it easier for the raters to follow your response.

The following is a list of common time sequencers that you can use, but avoid repeating the same ones throughout your response.

TIMELINE	TIME SEQUENCER
Beginning a story	First of all At first When this started/began When I arrived We first met at/when To start with # hours/days/weeks ago The other day

TIMELINE	TIME SEQUENCER
Directly following an action or event	And then And Next Which meant that After/Afterwards That/This caused _____ to happen Second/Third/Fourth, etc.
Passing longer periods of time	Later # hours/days/weeks later # hours/days/week earlier The following day/week/month A few / several days/hours passed Hours/Days/Weeks went by When we went back / returned
Concluding a story or ending an event	In the end Finally/Last That's why I _____ Overall As a result Because of this / Thanks to this

Activity 3A

Read the task below and then listen to the audio. Fill in the blanks with the time sequencers that were used.

Play **Unit 8 – Track 3.**

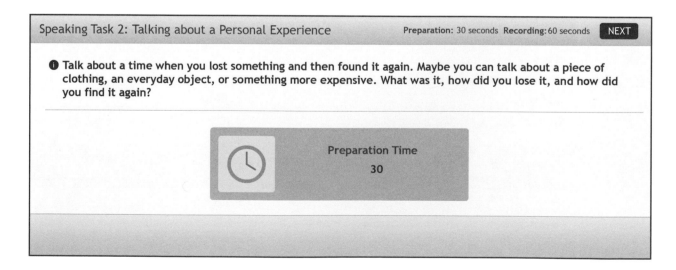

Speaking Task 2: Talking about a Personal Experience   Preparation: 30 seconds Recording: 60 seconds   NEXT

❶ Talk about a time when you lost something and then found it again. Maybe you can talk about a piece of clothing, an everyday object, or something more expensive. What was it, how did you lose it, and how did you find it again?

Preparation Time
30

1. _____, I went to have lunch with my husband, and the weather had turned very cold, and I was trying to find my only pair of gloves. I could not find them in the regular jacket pockets that I used to keep my gloves in, and so I felt worried that I'd lost my only pair of gloves plus the fact that I was panicking because I was going to be late. 2. _____ , I remembered that I'd actually worn a different jacket 3. _____ when it was cold at night, and I found those—my gloves. And I was incredibly happy because I didn't want my hands to be cold. And when I went to the restaurant, I let my husband know that I had found my gloves and how it felt—I felt relieved that I had found them because I didn't want to have to buy a new pair.

Activity 3B

Read this test taker's response and fill in each blank with one of the time sequencers from the table on the previous page.

So, I actually just lost my backpack 1. _____ at a Starbucks. I left to the washroom and when I came back, it was missing. So, I thought it was the barista who took it away 2. _____ I went to ask them if they had saw my backpack, and they said no. And so, I thought, "Oh, it must be someone else who took it away." 3. _____ I said, "Okay, if you happen to find it, would you please just give me a call?" And I left them with my phone numbers and my name. And I didn't expect to find it anyways, however, 4. _____ the Starbucks phoned me and said they found my backpack! I was, well, surprised and really happy. I went back to pick it up and it was still there, everything is inside, nothing's missed. It was a really really good experience to see how generous people are here in Canada. And, um, yeah, I love it!

Activity 3C

Listen to the audio of the sample response from the previous activity and compare the time sequencers used by the test taker with your answers in Activity 3B.
Play **Unit 8 - Track 4.**

Identifying Common Errors

The following are common errors that you should try to avoid when speaking. Avoiding these problems will make it easier for others to understand you and will help you perform at your best on the Speaking Test.

1. **Failing to Use Time Sequencers**

   Make sure you include time sequencing words to connect ideas in your answer. For Task 2, in particular, order the timing of events using a variety of sequencing words like "last week," "next," "after that," "then," "later," "finally," etc. Time sequencers will help raters follow the order of events in your response.

2. **Using Flat Intonation**

   Intonation refers to the rising and falling sound of your voice. English depends on variations in intonation to express meaning. Some test takers speak with little variation; their voices rarely go up or down, making it difficult for the raters to fully understand what they are saying. Do your best to use the rise and fall of your voice to express your thoughts and emotions.

3. **Using a Start-and-Stop Rhythm**

   Try to speak with a smooth rhythm. Avoid short, repetitive phrases—this can result in a start-and-stop rhythm which can make your response harder to follow.

Activity 4

In the space provided on the next page, identify examples of the three types of errors discussed in this section. This response may contain other types of errors, but for this activity, *only* focus on these three types of errors.

Play **Unit 8 - Track 5**.

Refer to the task in Activity 2A.

> The most memorable for me at the airport is when we go to fetch my sister who travelled for first time. She went to her summer camp at Morocco and we go there to fetch her with my whole family. We're happily waiting for her. Some doing things, some were doing different things, some are chatting around, some are excited, while others are doing other things. I see a lot of people around me and my family, that's why they need to. And that's the most memorable for me.

1. Failing to Use Time Sequencers

_____

_____

_____

2. Using Flat Intonation

_____

_____

_____

3. Using a Stop-and-Start Rhythm

_____

_____

_____

Self-Assessment

Use a device (phone, laptop, etc.) to record your response to this task and then play it back. Fill out the checklist as you listen. To practice timed responses for Speaking Task 2: Talking about a Personal Experience, give yourself **30 seconds** to prepare and **60 seconds** to speak.

Speaking Task 2: Talking about a Personal Experience	Preparation: 30 seconds Recording: 60 seconds NEXT

❶ Talk about a time when you had to make a fairly important decision. Maybe you can talk about a decision you had to make at work, or about your family, or about a change in your life. What was the decision about? Was the decision difficult or easy? How well did your decision turn out in the end?

Preparation Time
30

CELPIP SPEAKING CHECKLIST			
	Yes	**Sometimes**	**No**
1. Did you speak clearly with minimal pauses and hesitations?			
2. Did you use appropriate rhythm, pronunciation, and intonation?			
3. Did you accurately use a wide variety of words?			
4. Did you use time sequencers to show progression in your response?			
5. Did you avoid repeating ideas?			
6. Was your tone appropriate for the social context of the task?			
7. Was your response clearly organized?			
8. Was your response long enough?			
9. Did you fully address the task?			

Rate the Response

The following are sample responses to the task from the Self-Assessment activity.

1. Play each response and circle the appropriate CELPIP Level range from the given choices.
2. Write down some of the strengths and weaknesses of each response.
    *   You may wish to refer to the Performance Standards in Unit 6 to help you.
3. Check the Answer Key for an explanation of each response's level range.

Play **Unit 8 – Track 6.1**.

LEVEL M	LEVELS 3–4	LEVELS 5–6
Strengths:		
Weaknesses:		

Play **Unit 8 – Track 6.2**.

LEVELS 7–8	LEVELS 9–10	LEVELS 11–12
Strengths:		
Weaknesses:		

Play **Unit 8 – Track 6.3**.

LEVELS 7–8	LEVELS 9–10	LEVELS 11–12
Strengths:		
Weaknesses:		

UNIT
9
Describing a Scene

LEARNING FOCUS

- Providing an overview
- Describing the scene
- Using prepositions of place
- Using adjectives
- Describing actions
- Identifying common errors
- Self-assessment
- Rate the response

In Speaking Task 3: Describing a Scene, you will describe an image that is on the screen. One of the main challenges in this task is to describe the image as accurately as you can—including the locations of the various people and objects—and explain what you think is happening. Remember that the person to whom you are speaking cannot see the image.

... There are some p...
...ed shirt. In this scene. A few peopl...
...ding. Just behind the woman and her dog. ...
...d car. This scene shows many. I can see a number ...
...ere are some people next to the bus. There is a man ...
...In this scene. A few people are. To the right of the build...
...d the woman and her dog. To the left of the parked car...
...s many. I can see a number of people. There are som...
...to the bus. There is a man in a red shirt. In this sc...
...To the right of the building. Just behind the ...
...left of the parked car. This scene sh...
...le. There are some peo...
...n this...
...ding...

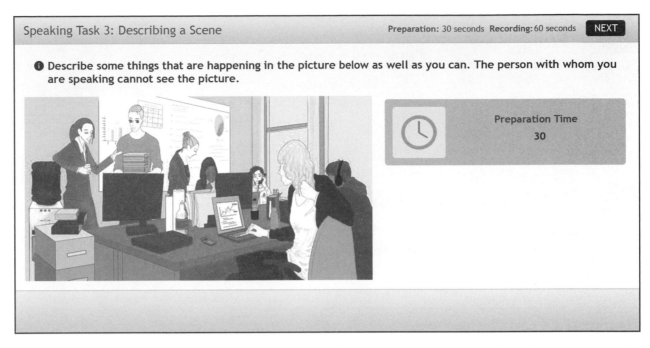

Speaking Task 3: Describing a Scene | Preparation: 30 seconds Recording: 60 seconds | NEXT

❶ Describe some things that are happening in the picture below as well as you can. The person with whom you are speaking cannot see the picture.

Preparation Time
30

Unit 9 – Image 1: This image is not displayed in full colour. See the original image online in the Focus LS Resource Portal.

Providing an Overview

In Speaking Task 3, you should begin your response with an overview (general description) of what is happening in the scene before you mention specific details. For example, you could mention the location, the main event, and the activity that most of the people are engaged in.

Activity 1

> Access the Focus LS Resource Portal for a full-colour version of this image.

Look at the image above and put a checkmark next to the statements that should be part of the overview.

☐ I see an office.

☐ A woman is standing by the water cooler talking to a co-worker.

☐ There are seven people working in the office.

☐ One guy is sitting in the corner listening to music on his headphones.

☐ They seem to be working on different tasks.

Describing the Scene

Once you have given your overview of the image, it's time to describe the details of what you see. There are many ways to approach describing the scene, but three important methods are

1. using prepositions to describe where people are,
2. using adjectives to describe what the people and objects look like, and
3. describing what actions the people are taking.

Using Prepositions of Place

Because this Speaking task tells you "the person with whom you are speaking cannot see the picture," it is important to describe where people are in relation to places, objects, and each other. Below is a list of some of the prepositions that can be used to help describe the location of people or objects.

above	behind	close (to)	in/inside	next (to)	overlooking
across (from)	beneath	distant (from)	in front of	on (top)	surrounding
among	beside	far (away/from)	in the middle	opposite	under
at	between	gathered around	near/by	over	underneath

Activity 2

Look at Image 1 again, and complete the following response with suitable prepositions of place from the chart above.

I can see a picture of an office with seven people doing different tasks. There's a lady leaning against a water cooler 1. _____ (*1 word*) the left side of the image. Standing 2. _____ (*1 word*) her is a blond guy in a red shirt who is holding a stack of papers. 3. _____ _____ (*2 words*) this man, 4. _____ (*1 word*) the right side of the image, are two women. One woman is wearing a purple and green shirt while the other has a purple and yellow shirt. They look like they are talking about something important. Sitting 5. _____ (*1 word*) them and the window is a guy in a white collared shirt who is talking on the phone. Directly 6. _____ _____ (*2 words*) him is a guy in a grey hoodie. It looks like he is listening to music. 7. _____ (*1 word*) him and sitting 8. _____ (*1 word*) the blond guy with the papers is a red-haired woman who is working on a report on her laptop.

Using Adjectives

If you look back at Activity 2, you will notice that much of the response involves describing people's appearances. In addition to using prepositions of place, you should use adjectives to identify the various people and objects in the image.

Refer to Image 1 once again. The phrase "the woman sitting at the desk" includes a preposition, but it isn't enough description to identify anyone in the image, since there are two women sitting down. Ambiguity like this can confuse the listener, who cannot see the image. Using adjectives helps clarify things.

One of the simplest ways to use adjectives is by describing people's appearances. For example, you could improve the above description and distinguish between the two women by doing the following:

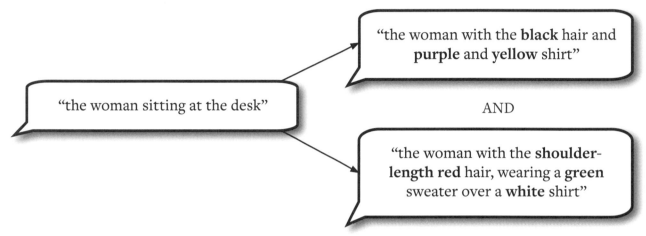

Activity 3

Look at Image 1 again, then rewrite the following phrases by adding at least one adjective. Make sure that you use different adjectives than those mentioned in Activity 2. The first one has been done for you.

1. the woman in the business suit _____ *the woman in the light blue business suit* _____

2. the man holding the papers _____

3. the man talking on the phone _____

4. the man wearing headphones _____

5. the woman in front of the whiteboard _____

Describing Actions

Describing people's actions is also an excellent way to describe the scene. When describing a person's actions, make sure you use the present progressive (is/are + verb-ing). The following activity will focus on this method.

Activity 4

Look at the image below and write each activity in the word box into the appropriate blank. The first one has been done for you.

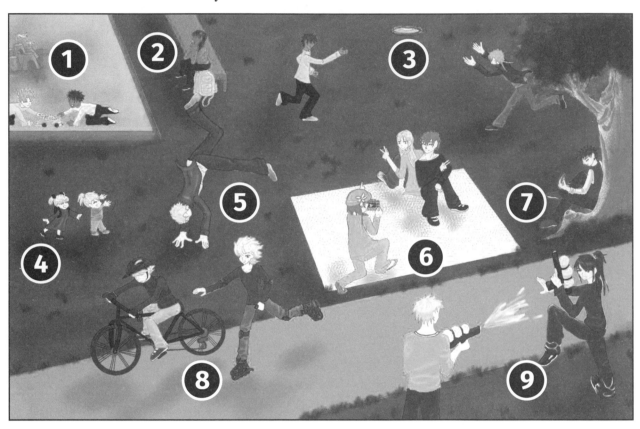

Unit 9 – Image 2: This image is not displayed in full colour. See the original image online in the Focus LS Resource Portal.

WORD BOX		
posing for photos	~~playing with a truck~~	racing each other
dancing together	having a water fight	leaning against a tree
doing a handstand	sitting on the bench	playing Frisbee

1. *playing with a truck*
2. _____
3. _____
4. _____
5. _____

6. _____
7. _____
8. _____
9. _____

Activity 5

Using what you have learned in Activities 2–4, write full sentences describing each numbered person/group in Image 2. Make sure to use prepositions, adjectives, and a description of the activity in each sentence. For example:

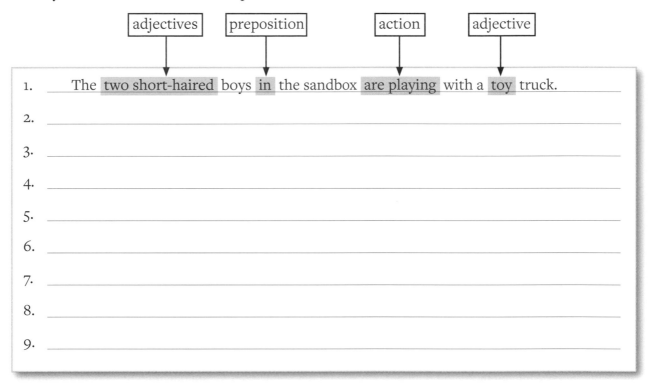

1.   The two short-haired boys in the sandbox are playing with a toy truck.

2.   _____

3.   _____

4.   _____

5.   _____

6.   _____

7.   _____

8.   _____

9.   _____

Identifying Common Errors

The following are common errors that you should try to avoid when speaking. Avoiding these problems will make it easier for others to understand you and will help you perform at your best on the Speaking Test.

1.   **Incorrect Word Choice**

     Be sure to use the correct words to describe the situation. For example, saying "I had a bad cough so I went to the **dentist**" when you really meant "I had a bad cough so I went to the **doctor**" could confuse the listener and possibly impact their understanding of the situation. This is especially important in Speaking tasks where the listener cannot see the image.

2.   **Misusing Verb Forms**

     The tense should be appropriate for the situation. For example, if you are talking about an action that is happening right now, use the present progressive ("he is running"). For Task 3, in particular, remember not to use the simple present ("he runs").

85

3. **Using Incorrect Subject-Verb Agreement**

   Be aware of whether the nouns you are using in your response are singular or plural, and make sure that you use the correct verb forms when referencing these nouns. For example, "there **are ten people** at the bus stop" is correct, whereas "there **is ten people** at the bus stop" is incorrect.

Activity 6

In the space provided below, identify examples of the three types of errors discussed in this section. This response may contain other types of errors, but for this activity, *only* focus on these three types of errors. Play **Unit 9 - Track 1**.

Refer to Image 2 for the corresponding Speaking task.

> Ok, seeing the picture, it's a, it's a park, and there are—so many kids are playing. And I can see there two kids in the ground—they are, they are little boy and they playing with a small car, and they trying to take from each other. There's a girl sitting on the desk and she looks very upset. There is a guy sitting under the tree. There is a guy jumping around, and there is two little girl watching, and I think they are clapping. There is a—there is a girl, and she's trying to pulling bicycle off another girl. And there's two girls sitting on the mat, and another girl taking their—

1. Incorrect Word Choice

   _____

   _____

   _____

2. Misusing Verb Forms

   _____

   _____

   _____

3. Using Incorrect Subject-Verb Agreement

   _____

   _____

   _____

Self-Assessment

Use a device (phone, laptop, etc.) to record your response to this task and then play it back. Fill out the checklist as you listen. To practice timed responses for Speaking Task 3: Describing a Scene, give yourself **30 seconds** to prepare and **60 seconds** to speak.

Unit 9 – Image 3: This image is not displayed in full colour. Access the original image online in the Focus LS Resource Portal.

CELPIP SPEAKING CHECKLIST	Yes	Sometimes	No
1. Did you speak clearly with minimal pauses and hesitations?			
2. Did you use appropriate rhythm, pronunciation, and intonation?			
3. Did you accurately use a wide variety of words?			
4. Did you begin by providing an overview of the scene?			
5. Did you use adjectives to accurately describe elements of the image?			
6. Did you accurately use prepositions of place for people and objects?			
7. Did you avoid repeating ideas?			
8. Was your response clearly organized?			
9. Was your response long enough?			
10. Did you fully address the task?			

Rate the Response

The following are sample responses to the task from the Self-Assessment activity.

1. Play each response and circle the appropriate CELPIP Level range from the given choices.
2. Write down some of the strengths and weaknesses of each response.
   - You may wish to refer to the Performance Standards in Unit 6 to help you.
3. Check the Answer Key for an explanation of each response's level range.

Play **Unit 9 – Track 2.1.**

LEVEL M	LEVELS 3–4	LEVELS 5–6
Strengths:		
Weaknesses:		

Play **Unit 9 – Track 2.2.**

LEVELS 7–8	LEVELS 9–10	LEVELS 11–12
Strengths:		
Weaknesses:		

Play **Unit 9 – Track 2.3.**

LEVELS 7–8	LEVELS 9–10	LEVELS 11–12
Strengths:		
Weaknesses:		

Making Predictions

LEARNING FOCUS

- Making predictions
- Organizing your response
- Identifying common errors
- Self-assessment
- Rate the response

In Speaking Task 4: Making Predictions, you will see the same image as the one that you saw in Task 3: Describing a Scene. However, this time, you will be asked to predict what you think will happen next within the image. One of the main areas of assessment in this task is your ability to use the proper grammatical form when making these predictions.

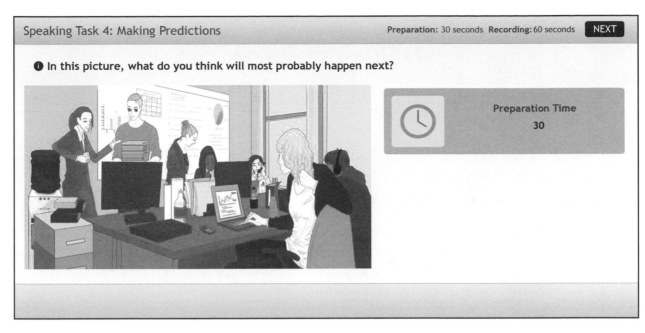

Speaking Task 4: Making Predictions   Preparation: 30 seconds Recording: 60 seconds NEXT

❶ In this picture, what do you think will most probably happen next?

Preparation Time
30

Unit 10 – Image 1: This image is not displayed in full colour. Access the original image online in the Focus LS Resource Portal.

Making Predictions

When you want to make a prediction, you can express yourself in a variety of ways. The following are three common grammar structures that you can use.

1. Subject + "will" + Verb
   - "He will begin working on a project."

2. Subject + "is/are going to" + Verb
   - "She is going to make a phone call."

> These two structures can be used to show that the action will happen sometime in the future.

3. Subject + "is/are about to" + Verb
   - "They are about to start a meeting."

> This structure tells your listener that the action will happen very soon.

Activity 1

Make a prediction about what each person in Image 1 will do next using "will," "is going to," or "is about to."

1. The man holding paper _____

   _____

2. The woman using a laptop _____

   _____

3. The woman sitting by the whiteboard _____

   _____

Continue ⬐➡

4. The man on the phone _____

_____

5. The man wearing headphones _____

_____

Organizing Your Response

For Speaking Task 3, you have to focus on providing detailed descriptions of what you see and how things and people are placed in the image. For Speaking Task 4, however, you only need to describe their locations as a way of identifying who or what you are talking about. This means you have a range of options for how to organize your response.

Some people like to organize their response by moving from left to right, top to bottom in the image; others prefer to move in a circle/spiral around the image (starting anywhere). The choice is yours.

Activity 2A

Look at the task below and complete the prediction for each person/activity using the left-to-right, top-to-bottom method. For this exercise, start in the top left corner and use the arrows as a guide. The first one has been done for you.

Unit 10 – Image 2: This image is not displayed in full colour. Access the original image online in the Focus LS Resource Portal.

1. The kids in the sandbox *will fight over the toy car.*

2. The woman sitting on the bench

3. The man about to catch the Frisbee

4. The girls dancing

5. The man doing a handstand

6. The people taking pictures

7. The man leaning against the tree

8. The kids racing down the path

9. The man and woman having a water fight

Tip The predictions you make should seem possible, based on what you see in the picture. Avoid making predictions that appear unrealistic.

Activity 2B

Look at the task below and complete the prediction for each person/activity using the circle/spiral method. Because this image is the same as in Activity 2A, do your best to come up with a different prediction for each person/activity.

Unit 10 – Image 3: This image is not displayed in full colour. Access the original image online in the Focus LS Resource Portal.

1. The kids in the sandbox _____

   _____

2. The woman sitting on the bench _____

   _____

3. The man about to catch the Frisbee _____

   _____

4. The man leaning against the tree _____

   _____

5. The man and woman having a water fight _____

   _____

Continue ➞

6. The kids racing down the path _____

    _____

7. The girls dancing _____

    _____

8. The man doing a handstand _____

    _____

9. The people taking pictures _____

    _____

Identifying Common Errors

These are common errors that you should try to avoid when speaking. Avoiding these problems will make it easier for others to understand you and will help you perform at your best on the Speaking Test.

1. **Making Unrealistic Predictions**

    Making a prediction that is unrealistic can negatively impact your score for Task 4. Your predictions should be about events that could happen next, based on the information within the image. For example, don't predict what the people in the image would do the next day or in a different location.

2. **Pausing**

    Long and frequent pauses can make it difficult for the listener to understand what you are saying. Such pauses can also make it seem like your vocabulary is limited, so, if possible, try to continue speaking throughout the duration of your response time.

3. **Interjecting**

    It is natural to use interjections (words like "um" and "ah") while you are speaking, but using these excessively can become distracting to the listener and make your speech difficult to follow.

Activity 3

In the space provided below, identify examples of the three types of errors discussed in this section. This response may contain other types of errors, but for this activity, *only* focus on these three types of errors.

Refer to Image 3 for the corresponding Speaking task.

> Play **Unit 10 - Track 1**.
> Access the audio via the Focus LS Resource Portal; the link is found in the Introduction.

> I-I-In this picture, like what I observe, I think uh the problem happen next is like uh, they were going to have some dinner for the . . . during the session once they are done with the playing and then the family comes and their kids, and then they will go for dinner. Uh, it will . . . Because in the park, they were, they were, the kids will enter a lot, and they go for some nice food in the restaurant. They can have any, like, order what they can have in the restaurant. After that, they go they want to go—to bed. Uh, most likely the picture is comes like ummm, uhh most probably happen next in the picture, like uh, y'know, and then there were red ones, you know, injuring a lot in the park. They will go, they going to . . .

1. Making Unrealistic Predictions

_____

_____

_____

2. Pausing

_____

_____

_____

3. Interjecting

_____

_____

_____

_____

Self-Assessment

Use a device (phone, laptop, etc.) to record your response to this task and then play it back. Fill out the checklist as you listen. To practice timed responses for Speaking Task 4: Making Predictions, give yourself **30 seconds** to prepare and **60 seconds** to speak.

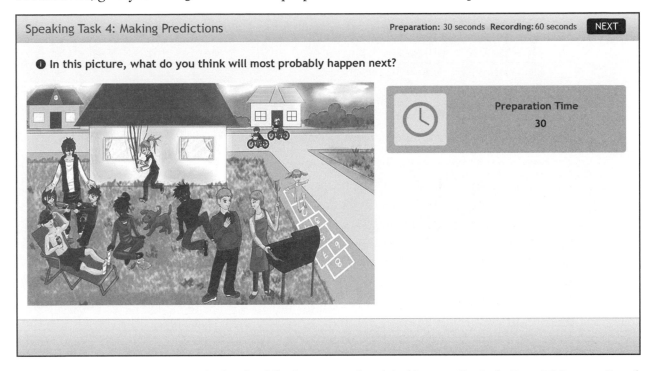

Unit 10 – Image 4: This image is not displayed in full colour. Access the original image online in the Focus LS Resource Portal.

CELPIP SPEAKING CHECKLIST	Yes	Sometimes	No
1. Did you speak clearly with minimal pauses and hesitations?			
2. Did you use appropriate rhythm, pronunciation, and intonation?			
3. Did you accurately use a wide variety of words?			
4. Did you avoid repeating ideas?			
5. Did you use the correct grammatical structure to make your predictions?			
6. Were your predictions about events that could logically happen?			
7. Was your response clearly organized?			
8. Was your response long enough?			
9. Did you fully address the task?			

Rate the Response

The following are sample responses to the task from the Self-Assessment activity.

1. Play each response and circle the appropriate CELPIP Level range from the given choices.
2. Write down some of the strengths and weaknesses of each response.
   - You may wish to refer to the Performance Standards in Unit 6 to help you.
3. Check the Answer Key for an explanation of each response's level range.

Play **Unit 10 – Track 2.1.**

LEVEL M	LEVELS 3–4	LEVELS 5–6
Strengths:		
Weaknesses:		

Play **Unit 10 – Track 2.2.**

LEVELS 7–8	LEVELS 9–10	LEVELS 11–12
Strengths:		
Weaknesses:		

Play **Unit 10 – Track 2.3.**

LEVELS 7–8	LEVELS 9–10	LEVELS 11–12
Strengths:		
Weaknesses:		

LEARNING FOCUS

- Understanding the format of Task 5
- Supporting your argument
- Brainstorming advantages and disadvantages
- Comparing advantages and disadvantages
- Identifying common errors
- Self-assessment
- Rate the response

In Speaking Task 5: Comparing and Persuading, you will compare different options, decide which is best, and persuade someone else of your choice. You will need to use descriptive language and comparative adjectives in order to support your choice. In addition to providing as many details as you can, it is essential to avoid only *describing* the options; you need to *compare* the two options and *persuade* your listener that your choice is more suitable. Remember to *directly* address the listener in this task.

option. Of these two
sense because. Not only is it chea
benefits to both, but I think. If we go with O
how much. I feel this is the best choice because.
sider. We should buy this because. I really think that
n. Of these two options, I think. Option A makes more s
Not only is it cheaper, it will also. There are benefits to
If we go with Option B, just consider how much. I feel
choice because. I'd like you to consider. We should
really think that the first option. Of these tw
kes more sense because. Not only i
ts to both, but I think
el th
ld

Speaking Task 5: Comparing and Persuading   Preparation: 60 seconds   NEXT

ⓘ You are getting married in the summer. Using the pictures and information, choose the location that you prefer. In the next part, you will persuade a family member that this is the best choice.

If you do not choose a location, the computer will choose one for you. You do not need to speak for this part.

Prince Edward Gardens

- $500 for a day
- Includes free parking
- 4 acres of flower gardens

The Sun Garden

- $800 for a day
- Includes tea and Chinese cakes
- 2 acres including house and gardens

Unit 11 – Image 1: This image is not displayed in full colour. Access the original image online in the Focus LS Resource Portal.

Speaking Task 5: Comparing and Persuading   Preparation: 60 seconds Recording: 60 seconds   NEXT

ⓘ Your fiancé's father wants to have the wedding in his backyard. Persuade your fiancé's father that the location you chose is better by comparing the two.

Your Fiancé's Father's Choice

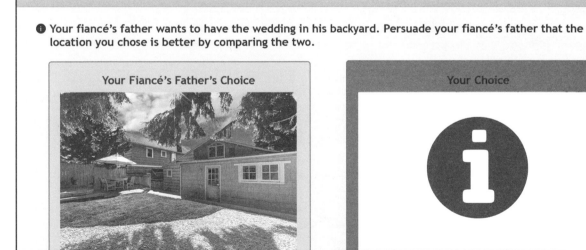

Fiancé's father's backyard

- One-quarter acre
- Free
- Family cooking for free

Your Choice

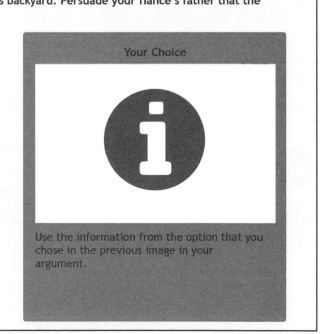

Use the information from the option that you chose in the previous image in your argument.

Unit 11 – Image 2: This image is not displayed in full colour. Access the original image online in the Focus LS Resource Portal.

Understanding the Format of Task 5

Speaking Task 5 is slightly different from other tasks in the Speaking Test because it takes place across two screens.

For the first screen, you will **not** speak; you will instead have 60 seconds to choose between two options. To make your selection, click on the option you want. It doesn't matter which option you choose, and the computer will select one for you if you do not click on an option.

For the second screen, you will need to compare your choice—which you clicked on in the first screen—with a new option and persuade your listener that your choice is better. For this screen, you will have 60 seconds to prepare your response, and 60 seconds to speak. Keep this format in mind while you practice for this task.

Supporting Your Argument

Speaking Task 5 draws upon your ability to compare and contrast ideas, so it's important to provide a logical explanation to support each point that you mention.

Imagine that you were trying to persuade your boss to purchase a new printer instead of new office chairs. Simply stating your preference, without supporting it with any reasons, is unlikely to convince her.

EXAMPLE: I think that we should buy a new printer for the office instead of new office chairs.

However, if you back up your choice with logical points of comparison, this can be much more persuasive.

EXAMPLE: I think that we should buy a new printer for the office. Our current printer is almost 5 years old and doesn't work half the time, but we just got new office chairs last year. In addition, purchasing a new printer would be slightly cheaper than buying new chairs.

> **Tip** It is fine to make up a name for the person to whom you are speaking. They do not need to be based on a real-life person.

Activity 1A

Identify whether each of the following is a weak or strong argument.

ARGUMENT	WEAK	STRONG
1. We should choose the typing workshop as we'll gain a skill that's useful not just in this job, but also for other activities outside of work.		
2. I think we should buy the red jacket for Susan. It is made of leather and costs $129.99.		
3. The French restaurant has a party room big enough to host our parents' wedding anniversary, so let's make a reservation there.		
4. Although the house in the suburbs is bigger, let's go with the seaside condo because it would allow us to jog and take long walks on the beach.		
5. I suggest that we stay at the hotel on Broadway. I've stayed there before. They have a restaurant in the lobby.		

Activity 1B

These two statements express opinions but are not supported by reasons. Rewrite these sentences by adding reasons that would help persuade someone to your point of view.

1. I recommend that you rent the apartment instead of the basement suite.

   _____

   _____

   _____

2. We should definitely take the shuttle bus from the airport.

   _____

   _____

   _____

Brainstorming Advantages and Disadvantages

One way to prepare your answer for Speaking Task 5 is to make a list of advantages that support your choice, and disadvantages that show why the other person's choice is either worse or not suitable.

Activity 2

Look at Image 1 and choose one of the two options being presented. You can spend about 1 minute making your choice.

Now look at Image 2. Spend a few minutes writing down the advantages of your choice from Image 1, and the disadvantages of the other option in Image 2 (your fiancé's father's choice). Write three or four points for each in the table below. Note that in the official test, you will have 1 minute to prepare.

ADVANTAGES (YOUR CHOICE)	DISADVANTAGES (FIANCÉ'S FATHER'S CHOICE)

Comparing Advantages and Disadvantages

Once you have listed the advantages and disadvantages of the options, you will need to compare them. To do this, you will need to use a range of grammar structures. For example:

1. "X is" + Comparative Adjective + "than Y"
   - Today is hotter than yesterday.
   - This TV is more expensive than that one.

2. "X is not as" + Adjective + "as Y"
   - The Falcon Lodge Motel is not as well-known as the Blueberry Hill Hotel.
   - This summer's weather forecast is not as extreme as last year's.

When you want to use the first grammar structure above, make sure to use the correct form of the adjective. The following table covers most rules for comparative adjectives.

ADJECTIVE RULES		
ADJECTIVE	**RULE**	**EXAMPLE**
1 syllable	Add "-er" to the end of the word.	Fast → Faster
1–2 syllables ending in "e"	Add "-r" to the end of the word.	Large → Larger
Other adjectives with 2 or more syllables	Add "more" or "less" in front of the adjective.	Boring → More boring Expensive → Less expensive
Adjectives ending in "y"	Change "y" to "i" and add "-er."	Happy → Happier
Irregular	Use the irregular form of the adjective.	Good → Better

Activity 3

The following response uses the Speaking Task 5 at the beginning of this unit. Listen to the response and fill in the missing comparative adjectives in the spaces provided.

> Play **Unit 11 - Track 1**.
> Access the audio via the Focus LS Resource Portal; the link is found in the Introduction.

> Father, I understand that you want to have a wedding in the back garden. However, my choice would be to have the wedding in Prince Edward Gardens for the following reason. Firstly, the gardens are much, much 1. _____ the backyard. More space actually is a benefit because the location includes free parking. That means we can invite all of the guests that we want to on our guest list and not worry about having to un-invite or not invite somebody. The other thing is that the location is a lot 2. _____. It's going to be a great setting for the photographs. The gardens include lots of different plants, shrubbery, and this will make for a much 3. _____ series of photographs after the wedding. Finally, the garden is so spacious you could also set up a tent that would accommodate people indoors if the weather wasn't as great. Although it's a little bit 4. _____, it would be a 5. _____ option than trying to squeeze everybody into the house if the weather was bad.

Identifying Common Errors

The following are common errors that you should try to avoid when speaking. Avoiding these problems will make it easier for others to understand you and will help you perform at your best on the Speaking Test.

1. **Using Empty Phrases**

   Test takers sometimes use words and phrases that do not help to express their ideas, that is, they are "empty" of meaning. Often, these words and phrases are repeated whenever the test taker is not certain what to say. If used too frequently, this can prevent the test taker from having enough time to fully develop their response. These words and phrases can also distract the listener from the purpose of the response. The following sentence illustrates this problem. "I, <u>like</u>, think we should, <u>like</u>, take the train because, like, it's much cheaper, <u>you know what I mean</u>?" Note that the underlined words and phrases do not make this sentence any more persuasive, and they are also quite distracting.

2. **Failing to Compare the Two Options**

   Remember that, in Task 5, you are attempting to persuade someone else that your choice is the best option. Some test takers describe each option without using comparative language to show how their choice is better. For example, if comparing two houses, it would not be enough to say, "This house costs $200,000 and has two garages. It has three bedrooms. The other house costs $20,000 and has no garage. There is one bedroom." It would be better to use comparative language to explain the difference between the two. For example, "Even though this house is more expensive, at $200,000, it is much bigger—it has three bedrooms rather than just one. It will also be much more convenient for us as it has two garages, which will be great since we both have cars. The other house doesn't even have one garage."

3. **Lacking Organized Structure**

   To effectively persuade your listener, it's important to structure your response in a logical way. It may be helpful, therefore, to briefly plan your response by selecting the main ideas you will be discussing before you start to speak. You could then begin your response by stating which option you chose, and follow up with a few reasons, based on the ideas you selected, to support your choice.

Activity 4

In the space provided below, identify examples of the three types of errors discussed in this section. This response may contain other types of errors, but for this activity, *only* focus on these three types of errors.
Play **Unit 11 - Track 2**.

Refer to Images 1 and 2 for the corresponding Speaking task.

> Uhh, I can choice uhh, the Sun Garden uh 800 for the day includes Chinese cakes, something like that, two acres include house and garden. It's good for me and quiet and nice. Uhhhhm. And good, everybody's gonna be okay. And I like so much noising and something like that. It's gonna be fun, uh the sun garden's is nice, I think so, for us. Very nice, location is good and everybody wants to see the uhh small lakes, something like that. It's better for us, I like that. We can choice, yeah. We can choose this.

1. **Using Empty Phrases**

_____

_____

_____

2. **Failing to Compare the Two Options**

_____

_____

_____

3. **Lacking Organized Structure**

_____

_____

_____

Self-Assessment

Use a device (phone, laptop, etc.) to record your response to this task and then play it back. Fill out the checklist as you listen. To practice timed responses for Speaking Task 5: Comparing and Persuading, give yourself **60 seconds** to make a choice between the first two options, **60 seconds** to prepare your response, and **60 seconds** to speak.

Speaking Task 5: Comparing and Persuading

Preparation: 60 seconds NEXT

You and three of your colleagues are going on a business trip from Toronto to New York. You found two suitable options. Using the pictures and information below, choose the option that you prefer. In the next section, you will persuade a colleague that your choice is the better choice.

If you do not choose an option, the computer will choose one for you. You do not need to speak for this part.

Going on an airplane

- $306 return per person
- travel time: 1 hour 25 minutes (plus 1-hour drive to airport)
- evening flights available

Taking the train

- $250 return per person
- travel time: 13 hours (plus 20-minute drive to station)
- train departs 8 a.m. and arrives 9 p.m.

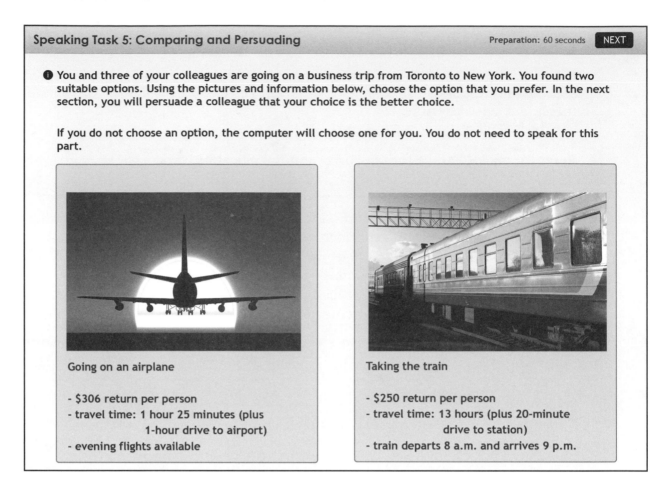

Unit 11 – Image 3: This image is not displayed in full colour. Access the original image online in the Focus LS Resource Portal.

Speaking Task 5: Comparing and Persuading

Preparation: 60 seconds **Recording:** 60 seconds NEXT

One of your co-workers is suggesting taking her car. Persuade this co-worker that the transportation you chose is more suitable by comparing the two.

Your Co-Worker's Choice

Going by car

- travel time: 7 hours
- $250 for gas
- can travel at any time

Your Choice

Use the information from the option that you chose in the previous image in your argument.

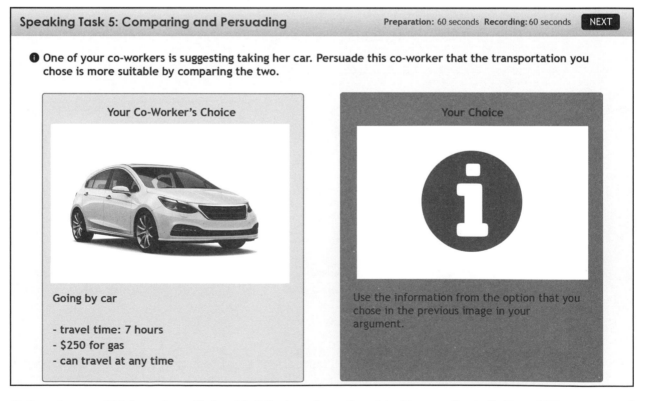

Unit 11 – Image 4: This image is not displayed in full colour. Access the original image online in the Focus LS Resource Portal.

CELPIP SPEAKING CHECKLIST			
	Yes	Sometimes	No
1. Did you address the listener directly?			
2. Did you speak clearly with minimal pauses and hesitations?			
3. Did you use appropriate rhythm, pronunciation, and intonation?			
4. Did you accurately use a wide variety of words?			
5. Did you avoid repeating ideas?			
6. Was your tone appropriate for the social context?			
7. Did you compare and contrast your choice with the other person's?			
8. Was your response clearly organized?			
9. Was your response long enough?			
10. Did you fully address the task?			

Rate the Response

The following are sample responses to the task from the Self-Assessment activity.

1. Play each response and circle the appropriate CELPIP Level range from the given choices.
2. Write down some of the strengths and weaknesses of each response.
   - You may wish to refer to the Performance Standards in Unit 6 to help you.
3. Check the Answer Key for an explanation of each response's level range.

Play **Unit 11 – Track 3.1**.

LEVEL M	LEVELS 3–4	LEVELS 5–6
Strengths:		
Weaknesses:		

Play **Unit 11 – Track 3.2**.

LEVELS 7–8	LEVELS 9–10	LEVELS 11–12
Strengths:		
Weaknesses:		

Play **Unit 11 – Track 3.3**.

LEVELS 7–8	LEVELS 9–10	LEVELS 11–12
Strengths:		
Weaknesses:		

UNIT 12

Dealing with a Difficult Situation

LEARNING FOCUS

- Making polite statements/requests
- Supporting your statement/request with reasons
- Identifying common errors
- Self-assessment
- Rate the response

Speaking Task 6: Dealing with a Difficult Situation presents you with a challenging scenario and two options for how to try to resolve it. You will choose one of these solutions and explain why you think it is the best choice. Two main areas of assessment in this task are your ability to provide reasons for your answer and your ability to change your word choice and tone depending on the context of the situation. Remember to *directly* address the listener in this task.

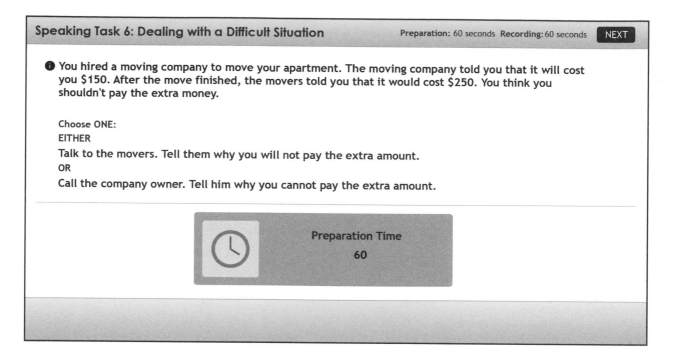

Speaking Task 6: Dealing with a Difficult Situation   Preparation: 60 seconds   Recording: 60 seconds   NEXT

ⓘ You hired a moving company to move your apartment. The moving company told you that it will cost you $150. After the move finished, the movers told you that it would cost $250. You think you shouldn't pay the extra money.

Choose ONE:
EITHER
Talk to the movers. Tell them why you will not pay the extra amount.
OR
Call the company owner. Tell him why you cannot pay the extra amount.

Preparation Time
60

Making Polite Statements/Requests

Speaking Task 6: Dealing with a Difficult Situation often involves convincing someone to change their mind or make a sudden change of plan. In such situations, you have a better chance of getting the outcome you want by expressing yourself in a polite way. Below is a list of some of the polite openings that you could use, as well as some examples of how to complete the statement or question.

POLITE OPENINGS	EXAMPLE
Excuse me . . .	. . . but could you please take shorter lunch breaks?
I feel really bad about this, but . . .	. . . I'd prefer it if you could take shorter lunch breaks.
I'm afraid to tell you this, but . . .	. . . I'd like it if you could take shorter lunch breaks.
I'm sorry to bring this up, but . . .	. . . you will need to take shorter lunch breaks.
It would mean a lot to me if . . .	. . . you took shorter lunch breaks.
I was hoping . . .	. . . that you could take shorter lunch breaks.
I wish you would . . .	. . . take shorter lunch breaks.
Maybe we could . . .	. . . discuss how long lunch breaks should be.
My suggestion is . . .	. . . that you should take shorter lunch breaks.
Sorry for the inconvenience, but . . .	. . . I'd like you to take shorter lunch breaks.
Unfortunately, . . .	. . . I'd prefer it if you could take shorter lunch breaks.
Would you be willing to . . .	. . . take shorter lunch breaks?
Would you consider . . .	. . . taking shorter lunch breaks?

Supporting Your Statement/Request with Reasons

If you make a demand or request without explaining yourself, people may feel confused or even a little upset. So, it is important to support your position with logical reasons.

Example:

SITUATION:	Your roommate refuses to help clean the apartment and is often quite loud. You are trying to get them to move out.
DIRECT STATEMENT:	Move out!
POLITE STATEMENT:	I wish you would consider finding somewhere else to live.
REASON:	I've talked to you so many times about helping clean the apartment, but you don't seem to have made an effort. In addition, our neighbours have complained several times about the volume of your music.

Activity 1

Rewrite each of the following sentences so that they are phrased more politely and then include at least one supporting reason.

1. **Direct Statement:** You must return the dog to the pet shop.

   a) **Polite Statement:** I'm sorry _____,

   but _____

   b) **Reason:** _____

   _____

2. **Direct Statement:** You have to sell your car.

   a) **Polite Statement:** I feel _____,

   but _____

   b) **Reason:** _____

   _____

3. **Direct Statement:** You must quit your job.

   a) **Polite Statement:** I'm afraid _____,

   but _____

   b) **Reason:** _____

   _____

Continue ⟶

4. **Direct Statement:** You can't go to work next week.

   a) **Polite Statement:** Would you consider _____

   _____

   b) **Reason:** _____

   _____

5. **Direct Statement:** You have to sign up for an exercise class.

   a) **Polite Statement:** Would you be willing _____

   _____

   b) **Reason:** _____

   _____

6. **Direct Statement:** I'm quitting your yoga class.

   a) **Polite Statement:** Sorry for _____ ,

   but _____

   b) **Reason:** _____

   _____

Activity 2A

Read the following task and underline three specific details that you can reference in your response. Note: In the Speaking Test, you should look for as many details as possible.

Speaking Task 6: Dealing with a Difficult Situation	Preparation: 60 seconds Recording: 60 seconds	NEXT

❶ You work for a big company. Your department is being asked to move to the other side of the office to make room for new employees. The new space is smaller and colder. Your co-worker is very upset about the move and wants to quit.

Choose ONE:
EITHER
Talk to your boss. Explain why your department should not move.
OR
Talk to your co-worker. Explain why he should not quit.

Preparation Time
60

Activity 2B

Think about how you can expand the response below by adding specific details and/or reasons to complete each idea. (Keep in mind that this exercise is focused on the first choice from the task on the previous page. On the official test, it does not matter which option you choose, as long as you discuss it convincingly.)

Excuse me, I was wondering if we could talk about the planned departmental move. I'm not

sure moving is the best idea _____

_____

_____ .

Also, if we move _____

_____

_____ .

Finally, I believe it's best if we _____

_____

_____

_____ .

Activity 2C

List three specific details this test taker used to help develop their response.

Play **Unit 12 - Track 1.**
Access the audio via the Focus LS Resource Portal; the link is found in the Introduction.

1	
2	
3	

Identifying Common Errors

The following are common errors that you should try to avoid when speaking. Avoiding these problems will make it easier for others to understand you and will help you perform at your best on the Speaking Test.

1. **Failing to Address the Listener Directly**

   As mentioned at the beginning of this unit, it is important to *directly* address the listener in Task 6. For example, it would be correct to say, "Listen, Tom, I understand how much you care about your dog, but it's just making too much noise." It would be incorrect to say, "I would tell Tom that I understand how much he cares about his dog, but it is just making too much noise."

2. **Expressing Incomplete Ideas**

   Make sure to fully explain each idea that you introduce. If you begin talking about one idea but don't fully explain it before moving to the next idea, this may make your response hard to follow. For example, it may confuse the listener if you said, "I have three ideas for the renovation. First, I really think we should . . . hmm . . . and it would also be good to add more parking spots . . ." It would be better to say, "I have three ideas for the renovation. First, I really think we should expand the lunch room. It would also be a good idea to add more parking spots. And lastly . . ."

3. **Using Words in the Wrong Order**

   In English, it is necessary to make sure that the words in your phrases and sentences are in the correct order. If some words are out of order, this can be confusing to the listener and may make your response harder to follow. For instance, "I **the took** train **work to** this morning" is incorrect, and the listener would have to work harder to figure out the meaning. "I **took the** train **to work** this morning" is correct.

Activity 3

In the space provided on the next page, identify examples of the three types of errors discussed in this section. This response may contain other types of errors, but for this activity, *only* focus on these three types of errors.
Play **Unit 12 - Track 2**.

Refer to the task in Activity 2A.

I think my co-worker, um, shouldn't be quit because, um, I try to convince him because the to work with this company it has a great benefits, and the bosses are good from here, and the same as all that like the employ the co-workers. And the most probably thing that I like it's like working with team together. They never leave you alone with any other problems that you have it, so I think that's what the people like it about this company, and the peoples are nice with the same nice age. They got big good and then this is the growest growing company at this point, so I think you shouldn't be quitting this job. I will try to talk with my boss together—

1. **Failing to Address the Listener Directly**

_____

_____

_____

2. **Expressing Incomplete Ideas**

_____

_____

_____

3. **Using Words in the Wrong Order**

_____

_____

_____

Self-Assessment

Use a device (phone, laptop, etc.) to record your response to this prompt and then play it back. Fill out the checklist as you listen. To practice timed responses for Speaking Task 6: Dealing with a Difficult Situation, give yourself **60 seconds** to prepare and **60 seconds** to speak.

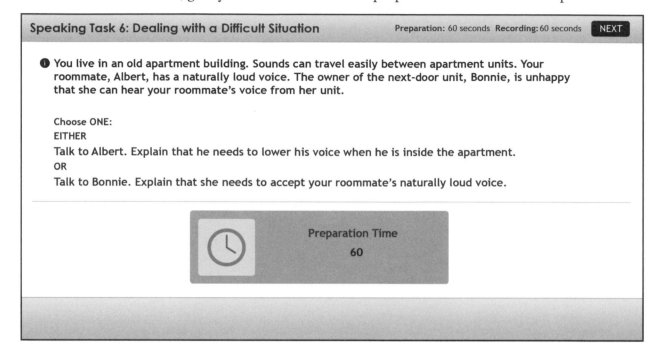

Speaking Task 6: Dealing with a Difficult Situation — Preparation: 60 seconds Recording: 60 seconds NEXT

ⓘ You live in an old apartment building. Sounds can travel easily between apartment units. Your roommate, Albert, has a naturally loud voice. The owner of the next-door unit, Bonnie, is unhappy that she can hear your roommate's voice from her unit.

Choose ONE:
EITHER
Talk to Albert. Explain that he needs to lower his voice when he is inside the apartment.
OR
Talk to Bonnie. Explain that she needs to accept your roommate's naturally loud voice.

Preparation Time
60

CELPIP SPEAKING CHECKLIST	Yes	Sometimes	No
1. Did you address the listener directly?			
2. Did you speak clearly with minimal pauses and hesitations?			
3. Did you use appropriate rhythm, pronunciation, and intonation?			
4. Did you accurately use a wide variety of words?			
5. Did you avoid repeating ideas?			
6. Was your tone appropriate for the social context?			
7. Was your response clearly organized?			
8. Did you use tactful words and phrases?			
9. Was your response long enough?			
10. Did you fully address the task?			

Rate the Response

The following are sample responses to the task from the Self-Assessment activity.

1. Play each response and circle the appropriate CELPIP Level range from the given choices.
2. Write down some of the strengths and weaknesses of each response.
   - You may wish to refer to the Performance Standards in Unit 6 to help you.
3. Check the Answer Key for an explanation of each response's level range.

Play **Unit 12 – Track 3.1**.

LEVEL M	LEVELS 3–4	LEVELS 5–6
Strengths:		
Weaknesses:		

Play **Unit 12 – Track 3.2**.

LEVELS 7–8	LEVELS 9–10	LEVELS 11–12
Strengths:		
Weaknesses:		

Play **Unit 12 – Track 3.3**.

LEVELS 7–8	LEVELS 9–10	LEVELS 11–12
Strengths:		
Weaknesses:		

Expressing Opinions

LEARNING FOCUS

- Expressing an opinion
- Developing your response using transitions
- Developing your response using word forms
- Identifying common errors
- Self-assessment
- Rate the response

In Speaking Task 7: Expressing Opinions, you will read a question about a common issue in society and then state your opinion about it. You are free to express any opinion that you like. You will be assessed on your ability to develop your response by providing supporting details and examples for your point of view.

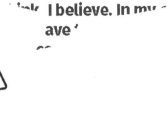

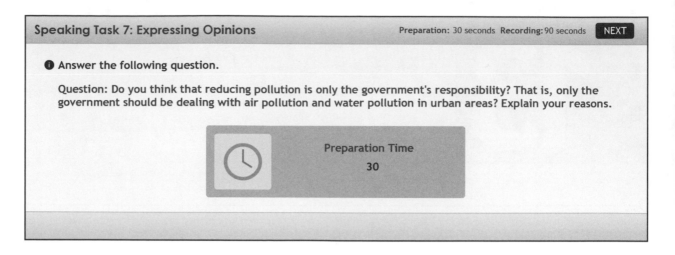

Speaking Task 7: Expressing Opinions   Preparation: 30 seconds Recording: 90 seconds   NEXT

ⓘ **Answer the following question.**

Question: Do you think that reducing pollution is only the government's responsibility? That is, only the government should be dealing with air pollution and water pollution in urban areas? Explain your reasons.

Preparation Time
30

Expressing an Opinion

In this Speaking task, you should do your best to state your position as clearly as possible at the beginning of your Recording Time. Here are some phrases that you could use to introduce your opinions:

- In my opinion . . .
- As far as I'm concerned . . .
- Personally, I think / I think that . . .
- I'd say that . . .
- I believe that . . .
- In my experience . . .

Sometimes test takers make small errors when using these expressions. In this activity, you will practice your ability to identify these common errors.

Activity 1

Read each of these statements in response to the task above. Then, circle the error(s) in the opinion phrase and rewrite it so that each is correct. The first question has been completed for you.

1. I am believing that a country's citizens should also help reduce their nation's pollution.

   I believe that

2. As far I'm concern, the government shouldn't be the only institution that's responsible for pollution control.

   _____

3. With my opinion, if everyone in the country tried their best to reduce how much they pollute, the environment would become much healthier.

   _____

Continue ⌐➤

4. On my experience, the government can only do so much to reduce pollution; you and I have to help with this as well.

5. I do say that government restrictions on pollution is the most effective way to help a country's air and water quality.

6. Personally, the only way to reduce the amount of pollution a country makes is if everyone takes responsibility for the pollution they create.

Developing Your Response Using Transitions

Using clear transitions between your ideas will help the raters follow the flow of your response. Being able to correctly use a variety of transitions can help improve the overall quality of your performance on the Speaking Test. The transitions that you use can be grouped by their purpose. Some of the most useful transitions and their categories appear in the activity below.

Activity 2A

Sort the transition words in the table into the correct categories on the next page. Check your answers in the Answer Key before proceeding to the next activity.

Transitions		
since	in comparison	therefore
specifically	yet	not only . . . but also
for example	if . . . then	both . . . and
moreover	consequently	while
similarly	however	to begin with
whereas	on one hand . . . on the other hand	first
but	because	for instance
finally	in other words	hence

CATEGORY	TRANSITIONS
GIVING EXAMPLES/ CLARIFYING	
SEQUENCING	
CAUSE/EFFECT	
ADDING INFORMATION	
EXPRESSING SIMILARITY	
CONTRAST	

Activity 2B

Complete the sentences by filling in the blanks with transition words/phrases from the table. Note that **not all** transitions in the table will be used, and some questions may have more than one possible answer.

1. It may be difficult to fund university degrees for every citizen _____ it would require increasing taxes by a large percentage.

2. Some parents _____ think that they always know what is best for their children _____ don't listen to their children or respect their independence.

3. Since it is so easy for people to hide their identities online, I think that _____ the teachers _____ the parents at my old school would not feel comfortable with the students having online-only friends.

Continue ⬋

4. Parents strongly believe that they have their children's best interests in mind; _____, their children believe that they have the right to choose how they wish to spend their free time.

5. _____, having friends online may allow someone who feels shy to socialize with other people; _____, face-to-face interaction is an important part of conversation because we communicate through body language as well.

Developing Your Response Using Word Forms

When you answer a Speaking question, it is important to demonstrate the full range of your vocabulary and avoid repetition. Although you should try not to repeat the same words, it can be an effective way of showing connections between your ideas to mention the same key word using different forms of that word. For example, in this paragraph, the word "repetition," a noun, is followed by the word "repeat," a verb, in the next sentence. These are different forms of the same word and, by using them together, it is possible to smoothly join ideas across two sentences. When using this strategy, consider the parts of speech that can be used with a particular word.

For example:

Creativity/Creativeness/Creation	Creative	Create	Creatively
(noun)	(adjective)	(verb)	(adverb)

Different forms of a word can be used to develop your ideas in a group of sentences.

Personally, I think learning some form of art is important for fostering **creativity** in a child. Music, painting, and dance are some artistic activities that children especially enjoy. Being **creative** allows people to come up with unorthodox ideas. Moreover, if someone can approach problems **creatively**, they will enjoy greater success in their careers.

Activity 3

Complete the response using the key word below. You will need to change the word form in each sentence so that it is grammatically correct.

KEY WORD: Know

Speaking Task 7: Expressing Opinions	Preparation: 30 seconds Recording: 90 seconds	NEXT

❶ **Answer the following question.**

Question: Parents think they know their children very well; children think they know themselves the best. What do you think? Please give your reasons.

I'd have to say that parents 1._____ their children best. This 2._____ comes from parents being able to watch their children grow and develop. Moreover, since parents have more life experience, they understand that children have only 3._____ themselves for the short time they have been alive. What I mean is, if children are young, they do not have a wide range of experiences that they can draw from. This makes 4._____ themselves almost impossible.

Activity 4

Now create your own response to the following Speaking task. Choose **two** (or more) of the key words below, and include **at least two** word forms of each in your response. Feel free to include more key words as well.

For the purpose of this activity, spend a few minutes brainstorming which key words and word forms you will include. Remember the Preparation Time for Task 7 is **30 seconds**.

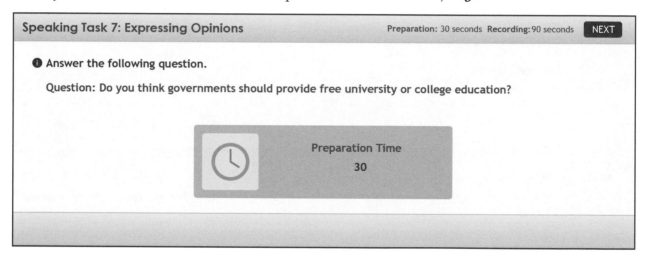

KEY WORDS	WORD FORMS
Pay	
Education	
Cost	
Attend	

Now, using a recording device (phone, laptop, etc.), record yourself speaking for **90 seconds** and then play it back. How many different key words/word forms were you able to use?

Identifying Common Errors

The following are common errors that you should try to avoid when speaking. Avoiding these problems will make it easier for others to understand you and will help you perform at your best on the Speaking Test.

1. **Misusing Uncountable Nouns**

    In English, nouns can be either countable or uncountable. Countable nouns have a singular and plural form and can be counted using numbers (one pen, five pens). Uncountable nouns are used for things that cannot be counted, such as liquids (milk) or abstract ideas (knowledge). These nouns do not have a plural form. For example, it is incorrect to say "I bought two **milks** yesterday" or "he has three **knowledges**." To express quantity in these cases, you will have to add a countable noun, such as "two **cartons** of milk," or an expression, like "**a lot of** knowledge." Make sure you use uncountable nouns correctly in your response.

2. **Failing to Provide Strong Reasons for Opinion**

    Whenever you are required to give your opinion, be sure to provide a few reasons supporting this opinion. Explain why you feel the way you do. It can also be helpful to explain why you do *not* feel a different way about the topic. If you do not provide any reasons for your opinion, or if your reasons are weak and unclear, this may make your response hard to follow.

3. **Failing to Follow All Directions**

    Read the instructions carefully. Note that some tasks will ask you to do more than one thing. Make sure that you have fully addressed the task.

Activity 5

In the space provided on the next page, identify examples of the three types of errors discussed in this section. This response may contain other types of errors, but for this activity, *only* focus on these three types of errors.

> Play **Unit 13 - Track 1.**
> Access the audio via the Focus LS Resource Portal; the link is found in the Introduction.

Refer to the Speaking task at the beginning of this unit.

> Ah, no, I disagree that it's not only the government's responsibility, but it's our responsibility too, as a people, as a responsible citizen because we can, we can, ah, keep our environment clean by cleaning up our houses . . . by cleaning up our neighbours' . . . putting garbages in the right places, and also using energy-efficient appliances in our houses. It will also reduce the pollution in the environment. Not using too much of a, uh, uh, uh, things that will cause the noise pollution. For example, not honking too much during driving, and also not listening to the loud music, mmm, uh, keeping everything, uh, keeping everything clean will help to grow a better clean environment.

1. **Misusing Uncountable Nouns**

    _____

    _____

    _____

2. **Failing to Provide Strong Reasons for Opinion**

    _____

    _____

    _____

3. **Failing to Follow All Directions**

    _____

    _____

    _____

 ## Self-Assessment

Use a device (phone, laptop, etc.) to record your response to this task and then play it back. Fill out the checklist as you listen. To practice timed responses for Speaking Task 7: Expressing Opinions, give yourself **30 seconds** to prepare and **90 seconds** to speak.

Speaking Task 7: Expressing Opinions

Preparation: 30 seconds Recording: 90 seconds `NEXT`

ⓘ Answer the following question.

Question: Do you think it's OK for high school students to have online friends, that is, friends they only know online? Give your reasons.

Preparation Time
30

CELPIP SPEAKING CHECKLIST	Yes	Sometimes	No
1. Did you clearly state your opinion at the beginning of your response?			
2. Did you speak clearly with minimal pauses and hesitations?			
3. Did you use appropriate rhythm, pronunciation, and intonation?			
4. Did you accurately use a wide variety of words?			
5. Did you avoid repeating ideas?			
6. Was your tone appropriate for the social context?			
7. Did you use appropriate transitions to develop your response?			
8. Was your response long enough?			
9. Did you fully address the task?			

Rate the Response

The following are sample responses to the task from the Self-Assessment activity.

1. Play each response and circle the appropriate CELPIP Level range from the given choices.
2. Write down some of the strengths and weaknesses of each response.
    *   You may wish to refer to the Performance Standards in Unit 6 to help you.
3. Check the Answer Key for an explanation of each response's level range.

Play **Unit 13 – Track 2.1.**

LEVEL M	LEVELS 3–4	LEVELS 5–6
Strengths:		
Weaknesses:		

Play **Unit 13 – Track 2.2.**

LEVELS 7–8	LEVELS 9–10	LEVELS 11–12
Strengths:		
Weaknesses:		

Play **Unit 13 – Track 2.3.**

LEVELS 7–8	LEVELS 9–10	LEVELS 11–12
Strengths:		
Weaknesses:		

Describing an Unusual Situation

LEARNING FOCUS

- Using descriptive vocabulary
- Developing your response
- Describing unfamiliar elements in the scene
- Identifying common errors
- Self-assessment
- Rate the response

In Speaking Task 8: Describing an Unusual Situation, you will describe an image of something unfamiliar. The person to whom you are speaking cannot see the image. One of the main challenges of this task is to adapt your vocabulary to describe a scene that may seem surprising or strange to you. Make full use of descriptive language to complete this task. It is essential to pay attention to the instructions because there are two parts. In the first part you will describe an image. In the second part there will be a follow-up task, such as inviting someone to join you in an activity that is depicted in the image. Remember to *directly* address the listener in this task.

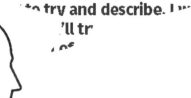

1. **Street Lamp**

   Simple Description: *large light on a metal pole*

   Detailed Description: *street lamp with a fluted bottom and a large bulb in a decorative casing*

2. **Cart/Carriage**

   Simple Description:

   Detailed Description:

3. **Cart roof/top**

   Simple Description:

   Detailed Description:

4. **Driver**

   Simple Description:

   Detailed Description:

5. **Megaphone**

   Simple Description:

   Detailed Description:

6. **Saddles**

   Simple Description:

   Detailed Description:

Activity 2A

In order to improve your performance on the Speaking Test, it is useful to consider things from the listener's perspective. Remember that in Task 8, the person with whom you are speaking cannot see the image, so you should make it as easy as possible for them to visualize the scene.

Listen to the following sample responses. Response 1 has a CELPIP Level range of 4–5, and Response 2 has a CELPIP Level range of 10–12. For the purpose of this exercise, you won't see the image, so as you listen, pay close attention to how it is described. You could even close your eyes to help you imagine what is being described.

Play Response 1 (**Unit 14 – Track 1**) and Response 2 (**Unit 14 – Track 2**).
Access the audio via the Focus LS Portal; the link is found in the Introduction.

Which response did you find easier to visualize?

Response 1 _____   or   Response 2 _____

Activity 2B

Listen to the tracks and add the missing information to the following chart, which compares the level of detail used in each response.
Play **Unit 14 – Tracks 1 and 2**.

TRACK 1	TRACK 2
• corner store has vegetable and fruits	• a corner store that basically sell fresh produce like fruit and vegetables • some of the vendors, the people selling the fruit and the vegetables
• outside the city street	• _____ • a place where farmers would live
• _____	• a big banner that says "Fresh Fruits" on my left-hand side
• another building in front of the corner store • with red roof	• _____

Both responses generally mention the same points, but Response 2 uses a wider and more precise range of vocabulary to describe the scene. Note that there were many other factors that contributed to the score of each response, but the use of descriptive language was certainly one of them.

Developing Your Response

Remember that to score well in Speaking Task 8, you need to include a wide range of details to make your response as descriptive and as well developed as possible. To do that, it is helpful to ask yourself questions to plan your response. The following list is a good starting point but does not contain all possible questions. It is not necessary to answer all of these questions, and some might not be useful in every situation.

- Who am I talking to?
- Is the scene inside or outside?
- What is the time of day in the picture?
- What is/are the main object(s)?
- What shape(s) is/are the main object(s)?

- Are there any people?
- What is the season?
- What is/are the main object(s) used for?
- What colour(s) is/are the main object(s)?
- What is/are the material(s)?

Activity 3A

Look at the task below and create notes, using the "Questions to Ask Yourself" column in the following chart as a guide. Remember, not all of the questions will be applicable to this activity. The first row has been completed for you.

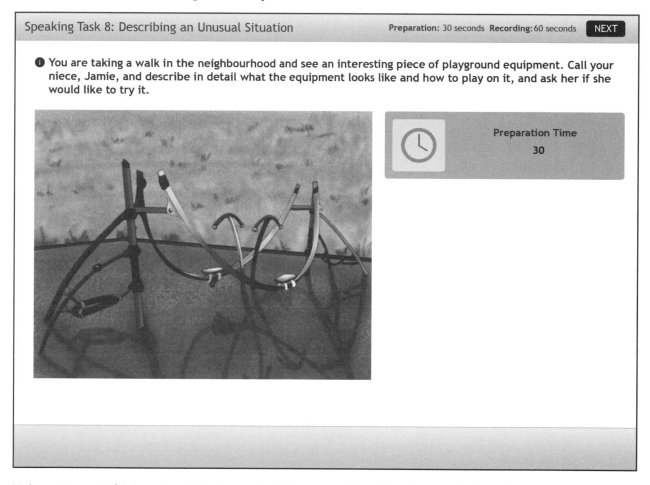

Speaking Task 8: Describing an Unusual Situation | Preparation: 30 seconds Recording: 60 seconds | NEXT

ⓘ You are taking a walk in the neighbourhood and see an interesting piece of playground equipment. Call your niece, Jamie, and describe in detail what the equipment looks like and how to play on it, and ask her if she would like to try it.

Preparation Time
30

Unit 14 – Image 2: This image is not displayed in full colour. Access the original image online in the Focus LS Resource Portal.

QUESTIONS TO ASK YOURSELF	NOTES
Who am I talking to?	*Jamie, niece*
Are there any people?	
Is the scene inside or outside?	
What is the season?	
What is the time of day in the picture?	
What is/are the main object(s) used for?	
What shape(s) is/are the main object(s)?	
What colour(s) is/are the main object(s)?	
What is/are the main object(s)?	
What is/are the material(s)?	

Describing Unfamiliar Elements in the Scene

Task 8 is similar to Task 3 in that you are asked to describe an image. However, rather than being presented with a familiar image, such as a classroom or a park, you will be presented with an unusual scene. Although it may be unfamiliar, there may be parts that resemble something that *is* familiar to you. Therefore, it is a useful strategy to compare aspects of the image to something else. This can be particularly helpful if you can't find the vocabulary to precisely describe the image.

Activity 3B

Look at the image in Activity 3A once more. What does the image look like to you? What is a similar object or situation that you can compare it to?

Now play the following two excerpts from high-level responses. Each response describes the image by comparing it to something else. Listen to each response and then write down what the test taker is comparing the image to.

1. Play **Unit 14 – Track 3**. What is the image being compared to? (*Hint: furniture and theme park*)

_____

2. Play **Unit 14 – Track 4**. What is the image being compared to? (*Hint: hanging bed*)

Activity 3C

Use a device (phone, laptop, etc.) to record your response to the task in Activity 3A using the descriptive notes you have written. Remember to make comparisons to other objects or situations if you are struggling to describe the image. Try to speak for 60 seconds.

Then, play back your response and consider the following: Did you use detailed descriptive language? Did your response include answers to some of the questions from Activity 3A? Did you compare the scene to anything that was more familiar to you? If so, did you find it easier to describe things that way?

Play **Unit 14 – Track 5** for a high-level response to this task (CELPIP Level range 10–12).

Identifying Common Errors

The following are common errors that you should try to avoid when speaking. Avoiding these problems will make it easier for others to understand you and will help you perform at your best on the Speaking Test.

1. **Misusing Prepositions**

   There are numerous prepositions in English, even just to describe location. Many test takers struggle with using the correct prepositions when describing elements of an image. Using an incorrect preposition may cause the listener to misunderstand your description. For example, "the dog **in** the car" and "the dog **on** the car" describe two very different situations.

2. **Going Off Topic**

   It's important to stay focused on exactly what you are being asked to do in each Speaking task. Make sure everything you say contributes to the development of your response. Avoid talking about things that are not related to the task. Remember that whenever you go off topic, you are losing time in which you could be developing your main ideas.

3. **Using Imprecise Language**

   Using precise language in your response will make it easier for the listener to understand what you are discussing. For example, saying "there's this colourful thing stuck in a tree" would make it very hard for the listener to understand what you are describing. "There's a red, purple, and blue rectangular object stuck in a tree—I think it's a kite" would be much easier to understand because the language is more precise. This is especially important in Task 8 because you will need to use very precise language in order for the listener to imagine this unusual situation.

Activity 4

In the space provided below, identify examples of the three types of errors discussed in this section. This response may contain other types of errors, but for this activity, *only* focus on these three types of errors.

Play **Unit 14 - Track 6**.

Refer to Image 2 for the corresponding Speaking task.

> Hello Janie—Hello Jamie (sorry). Uh, I was running on the park, and I saw, I remember, I just remembered you at the moment I saw what is a quite big equipment. The, the municipal put it on the park, which let you have some exercise. It's very common, I think it's very common in this area and you saw more frequently. It's quite the oval, it's look like what we would sit on, what we play in, of this jumpings, you remember? I remember that was accident. And so it's very similar to this—of a full structure, a wall structure to do it. And you can sweep it, and you can hold it in different ways. But I think it's, you're going to enjoy it. If you, at the moment you see it, you're start to remember what was kid—

1. **Misusing Prepositions**

   _____

   _____

   _____

2. **Going Off Topic**

   _____

   _____

   _____

3. **Using Imprecise Language**

   _____

   _____

   _____

Self-Assessment

Use a device (phone, laptop, etc.) to record your response to this prompt and then play it back. Fill out the checklist as you listen. To practice timed responses for Speaking Task 8: Describing an Unusual Situation, give yourself **30 seconds** to prepare and **60 seconds** to speak.

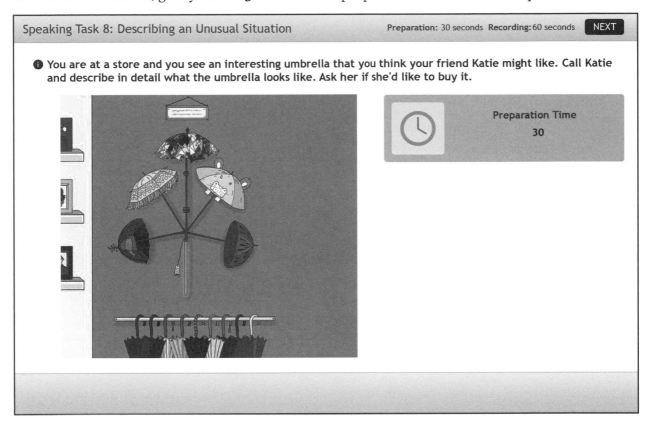

Unit 14 – Image 3: This image is not displayed in full colour. Access the original image online in the Focus LS Resource Portal.

CELPIP SPEAKING CHECKLIST	Yes	Sometimes	No
1. Did you address the listener directly?			
2. Did you speak clearly with minimal pauses and hesitations?			
3. Did you appropriate rhythm, pronunciation, and intonation?			
4. Did you accurately use a wide variety of words?			
5. Did you avoid repeating ideas?			
6. Was your tone appropriate for the social context?			
7. Was your response clearly organized?			
8. Was your response long enough?			
9. Did you fully address the task?			

Rate the Response

The following are sample responses to the task from the Self-Assessment activity.

1.   Play each response and circle the appropriate CELPIP Level range from the given choices.
2.   Write down some of the strengths and weaknesses of each response.
     *   You may wish to refer to the Performance Standards in Unit 6 to help you.
3.   Check the Answer Key for an explanation of each response's level range.

Play **Unit 14 – Track 7.1**.

LEVEL M	LEVELS 3–4	LEVELS 5–6
Strengths:		
Weaknesses:		

Play **Unit 14 – Track 7.2**.

LEVELS 7–8	LEVELS 9–10	LEVELS 11–12
Strengths:		
Weaknesses:		

Play **Unit 14 – Track 7.3**.

LEVELS 7–8	LEVELS 9–10	LEVELS 11–12
Strengths:		
Weaknesses:		

LISTENING – UNIT 1

Activity 1

1. General Meaning
Explanation: This question requires an overall understanding of the passage, so it is general meaning.
2. Inference
Explanation: The woman does not specifically state why she is finding the cab, so this is an inference.
3. Specific Details
Explanation: The woman explains that she really liked the coat; this is a specific detail from the passage.

Activity 2

1. a) A conversation
   Explanation: The passage is a conversation, since three of the screens say, *"You will hear a conversation."*
   b) Two speakers
   Explanation: There are two speakers, because the instructions that describe the Listening part say, *"You will hear a conversation between a woman and a man."*
   c) In a store
   Explanation: The conversation takes place in a store, since the instructions say, *"The man is an employee at a store and the woman is a customer."*
   d) Three sections
   Explanation: The first instruction screen says, *"You will hear a conversation in 3 sections."*
   e) About 1 to 1.5 minutes
   Explanation: The listening passage is 1 to 1.5 minutes long, since the information above the audio recording says, *"It is about 1 to 1.5 minutes long."*

2. a) A conversation
   Explanation: The passage is a conversation, since three of the screens say, *"You will hear a conversation."*
   b) Two speakers
   Explanation: There are two speakers, because the instructions that describe the audio say, *"The conversation is between two co-workers."*
   c) N/A
   Explanation: This is not answerable from the given information. However, this is still a good question to keep in mind when previewing.
   d) One section
   Explanation: The first instruction screen says, *"You will hear a conversation followed by 5 questions."* This means there is only one section in the audio.
   e) About 1.5 to 2 minutes
   Explanation: The listening passage is 1.5 to 2 minutes long, since the information above the audio recording says, *"It is about 1.5 to 2 minutes long."*

3. a) A discussion
   Explanation: The passage is a discussion, since the instructions say, *"You will watch a discussion."*
   b) Three speakers
   Explanation: There are three speakers, because the instructions that describe the video say, *"You will watch a discussion between three co-workers."*
   c) At a rollerblade rental shop
   Explanation: The conversation takes place in a rollerblade rental shop since the instructions say, *"They are colleagues at a rollerblade rental shop."*
   d) One section
   Explanation: The first instruction screen says, *"You will watch a 2-minute video. Then 8 questions will appear."*
   e) About 2 minutes
   Explanation: The video is 2 minutes long, since the information in the introduction says, *"You will watch a 2-minute video."*

LISTENING – UNIT 2

Activity 1

1. Two
Explanation: The fact that there are two speakers can be found by listening to the passage.

2. D
Explanation: There are no specific details that provide the answer in the passage. However, the other choices do not make sense from the dialogue. The speakers are not strangers because the man uses the woman's first name. The speakers are not necessarily co-workers because the man hasn't worked in a dance company before, while the woman has experience in this area. The speakers are not necessarily classmates because the conversation does not include references to classes or schools. Therefore, the speakers are probably friends.

3. A
Explanation: The speakers are familiar with each other, as demonstrated through the use of the woman's first name and their informal use of language, such as, "*I mean, what do they want to see*" and "*I wouldn't.*"

Activity 2

1. the woman's disappointment about the performance
Explanation: "That" refers not to a specific object, but to the concept the woman is conveying: that she was disappointed in the performance.

2. the coat check number
Explanation: This is the correct answer because the man asks, "Could I have your number please?" prior to the woman's statement.

3. the coat
Explanation: "It" is referring to the woman's coat, as mentioned by the man in the previous statement in the conversation.

Activity 3A

1. B
Explanation: In the audio, the woman asks, "could you please look again?" in reference to the coat. In Option B, when the man says, "yes, I will," he is directly responding to the woman's request. In support of this, when he says, "I'm sure I'll be able to find **it**," the "it" refers to the woman's coat, since she previously said, "I really like that **coat**."

2. A
Explanation: The man returned the woman's coat to her during the audio—in Option A, the woman is expressing relief because she's happy to have the coat back. "Where was **it**" again refers to her coat, which the man mentioned previously.

3. A
Explanation: In the audio, the man explains that there was a mix-up since "the other attendant must have mistaken" her coat for a similar one. In Option A, the woman is expressing her disappointment at the problem caused by the attendant because she really likes her coat, and she wishes to complain about the inconvenience.

4. B
Explanation: In the audio, the woman mentions that she will be more understanding about the attendant's mistake, but she also mentions, "I missed my **cab**." In Option B, the attendant uses the opportunity to help her and to satisfy her as a customer. When he says, "I'll call you another **one**," "one" refers to another cab.

Activity 3B

1. A	3. B	5. B	7. C
2. D	4. C	6. A	8. D

Activity 3C

1. Closing   2. Opening

Activity 3D

OPENING	CLOSING
Track 5.1	Track 5.4
Track 5.2	Track 5.3

Activity 3E

OPENING	CLOSING
Track 6.1	Track 6.5
Track 6.6	Track 6.3
Track 6.2	Track 6.4

Activity 4

	CONTRACTION	FULL FORM
1.	What's	What is
2.	It's	It is
3.	Doesn't	Does not
4.	Wouldn't	Would not
5.	You're	You are
6.	Isn't	Is not
7.	Don't	Do not
8.	Don't	Do not
9.	They're	They are
10.	You're	You are
11.	I'll	I will
12.	Aren't	Are not
13.	I'm	I am
14.	Aren't	Are not
15.	There's	There is*
16.	They're	They are
17.	I'm	I am
18.	Don't	Do not
19.	Wouldn't	Would not
20.	Don't	Do not
21.	Doesn't	Does not
22.	That's	That is
23.	Don't	Do not
24.	That's	That is

* The contraction in this instance ("when **there's** kids") is grammatically incorrect; it should be "where **there're** kids" or simply "when **there are** kids." Errors like this are fairly common in informal speech, however, and the purpose of this activity is to practice recognizing contractions—regardless of their use.

Activity 5

Example notes; answers may vary.

SPEAKER 1: MAN	SPEAKER 2: WOMAN
Who: man = employee	**Who:** woman = co-worker
What: Wants to ask quest'n Wants to buy someth'g special Maybe hockey tix Boss ≠ like theatre Likes cook'g, cards, swim'g Agrees, will buy tix to cook'g event Keep flyer?	**What:** Quest'n about rltnshps? Get gift card? Go 2 theatre? Tix 2 cooking event w/ famous chef
When: ?	**When:** ?
Where: @ office?	**Where:** @ office?
Why: Boss will rctirc, and wants to buy him gift	**Why:** Y buy gift if employees will buy together?

Test Practice

Track 9

1.	A	3.	A	5.	A	7.	B
2.	D	4.	C	6.	D	8.	B

Track 10

1.	B	3.	A	5.	A
2.	C	4.	B		

Track 11

1.	C	3.	D	5.	A
2.	C	4.	D	6.	B

LISTENING – UNIT 3

Activity 1A

1. A (separate ideas)
Explanation: This pause is separating the idea of *when* the event occurred ("on Friday") from *what happened* ("instead of getting a bag of hot chicken . . ."). In writing, this would be shown with a comma.

2. C (emphasize important words)
Explanation: There is a pause separating each word in the phrase "cold hard cash." This shows that these three words are being emphasized.

3. B (indicate extra information)
Explanation: The pauses separating "a third-year law student at the University of Toronto" from the rest of the audio show that this is extra information, and that the sentence can be understood without it. For example, "Richard Coleman pulled up to the drive-thru window of the popular Charlie's Chicken restaurant . . ."

4. A (separate ideas)
Explanation: The pause here is separating two ideas and is acting like a period in writing.

5. A (separate ideas)
Explanation: The pause here is separating the explanation of what happened (". . . bundle of cash instead") from Coleman's words ("I couldn't believe it!").

Activity 1B

1. Excuse me, which way is the train station? ↘
2. We have a meeting today, right? ↘↗
3. Are you going to Sasha's graduation? ↗
4. I think we should go that way. ↘
5. Have you ever been to the theatre? ↘↗
6. Have you seen the Celebration of Lights? ↗

Activity 1C

If we want to make it for the **4 o'clock** ferry to Vancouver **Island**, we will need to **arrive** at the terminal **before 3 o'clock**. So, **please** try to **be ready** to leave by 2.

Last **Friday, visitors** to the **Bridal Falls park** received a **welcome surprise**. **Actors** in **Victorian costumes** presented a **traditional** travelling **tea service**. **Guests** were **treated** to **fresh pastries**, **sandwiches**, and **three varieties** of **local tea**.

Activity 2

See bolded words; answers may vary slightly. The idea of "Ontario resident" occurs at other times in the form of "he," "Richard Coleman," and "Coleman." The idea of fast food appears numerous times by being referred to as "a bag of hot chicken," "chicken burger and french fries," and "chicken burger." The ideas of a bag and cash are also very important since "bag" appears three times, and "cash" appears twice.

The repetition of these terms suggests that the general topic of this passage is about Richard Coleman and a bag of money at a fast food restaurant.

> An **Ontario resident** ordered some **fast food** on Friday, but instead of getting a **bag** of hot **chicken**, he got a **bag** of cold hard **cash**. **Richard Coleman**, a third-year law student at the University of Toronto, pulled up to the drive-thru window of the popular Charlie's **Chicken** restaurant on Broadway and ordered a **chicken burger and french fries** to go. At the first stoplight on his way home, **Coleman** reached inside the take-out **bag** for his **chicken burger** and pulled out a bundle of **cash** instead.

Activity 3

1. General Meaning
C
Explanation: The answer is "a scam targeting the elderly." We know this because the passage includes the following information:

- "The bank issued a statement after a clerk discovered suspicious charges against the account of Mary Bryce . . ."
- "It turned out she had been paying a bill of $20 to an unknown payee every month for 4 years without being aware of it."
- "Mary suspects that her husband might have been contacted over the phone years ago and convinced to sign up for the service."
- "However, seniors remain highly susceptible to financial scams due to lack of up-to-date knowledge."

This question requires you to listen for general meaning and identify which ideas are part of the main topic, and which are details.

2. Specific Detail
A
Explanation: The answer is "help seniors become more vigilant." We know this because the passage includes

the following information:

- "Free workshops educate older citizens on financial abuse, fraud, and cash management during retirement."

This question requires you to listen for specific details and identify the answer that says the same thing using different words.

3. Specific Detail

B

Explanation: The answer is "was incredibly beneficial." We know this because the passage includes the following information:

- "Mary Bryce already took the course and found it extremely informative and practical."

This question requires you to listen for specific details and identify the answer that says the same thing using different words.

4. General Meaning

C

Explanation: The answer is "dishonest phone marketing." We know this because the passage includes the following information:

- "discovered suspicious charges"
- "an unknown payee"
- "husband might have been contacted over the phone years ago"

What's important here is to recognize that you need to pull ideas from more than one place in the passage to find the right answer. The three ideas mentioned above need to be added together to be able to choose the correct answer.

Activity 4A

Specific lengths of answers may vary.

1. Earlier today
2. As Monica LeBlanc was monitoring the security cameras at Mason's Department Store
3. Two hours later
4. earlier
5. Within the hour
6. now

Activity 4B

5	a. Authorities are **now** trying to determine the motive for the crime.
2	b. **As Monica LeBlanc was monitoring the security cameras at Mason's Department Store**, she noticed a man behaving erratically in one of the aisles.
1	c. **Earlier today**, a security guard thwarted a kidnapping attempt by providing police with information that led to the rescue of a young girl.
3	d. **Two hours later**, police put out an amber alert that a seven-year-old girl had been abducted
4	e. **Within the hour**, police apprehended the man as he was speeding out of the city

Activity 6

Example notes; answers may vary.

Who?	Alan Cameron = driver	Samantha Park = city spokesperson
What?	No one ready 1st snowfall Chaos on roads Blizzard Afraid of being hit ♂	City City = prepared 4 snowstorms ♀ 30 trucks on road ♀ Stuck on road 4 2hrs ♂
When?	Nov 19	Morn'g commute
Where?	Halifax, Nova Scotia	
Why?	Black ice common Cars were slid'g on road ♂	Salt trucks ≠ drive ∴ traffic ♀

Test Practice

1. B   3. A   5. C
2. A   4. D

LISTENING – UNIT 4

Activity 1

1. C

Explanation: "in a kitchen" is correct because of the dishwasher and other kitchen appliances in the background.

Activity 2

1. C   2. B   3. B

Activity 3

1. D   3. C   5. B
2. A   4. E

Activity 4A

Negative	Neutral	Positive
Quarrel	Discussion	Agreeable
Terrible	Debate	Terrific
Boring	Sufficient	Intriguing
Forgettable	Moderate	Memorable
Unreasonable	Acceptable	

Activity 4B

1. Video 1.1   Positive   3. Video 1.3   Negative   5. Video 1.5   Neutral
2. Video 1.2   Negative   4. Video 1.4   Negative

Activity 5

Example notes; answers may vary.

WH Word	ANGELA (SPEAKER 1)	JED (SPEAKER 2)	RONALDO (SPEAKER 3)
Who	Worker	Worker	Worker
What	NA Ins Conf = postp'n'd Cmpy 2 chng resv Schedule emerg meeting	Trvl early Why learn late Cancel conf? Wants more info	C'mp'y made resv > 1000 ppl attending conf Taking fam 4 Easter, 1wk Reschedl clients Make conf optional? Thinks sessions = boring
When	Afternoon		3 wks away
Where	Florida		
Why	Big --> need --> space Hotel = mistake Knows b/c outside mngr office	Give prsntn Wants = relaxed	Wants warm Easter, not cold

Test Practice

1. B   4. C   7. D
2. A   5. A   8. D
3. D   6. C

LISTENING – UNIT 5

Activity 1

1. claims
2. argues
3. believes
4. suggests
5. talks
6. points out

Activity 2

1. fact
2. opinion
3. opinion
4. fact
5. opinion
6. opinion
7. opinion
8. fact

Activity 3

1. A

Explanation: According to the passage, Bennett thinks "that foreseeable consequences are not the only motivating factor. She suggests that many people consider illegal downloading to be a victimless crime." Therefore, A is correct.

2. B

Explanation: According to the passage, "Ethan Miller points out [that] these companies were built on the backs of internet pirates. They take our basic desire for immediate entertainment and allow us to circumvent the risk of potential fines and lawsuits." Thus, B is correct.

Activity 4

1. D

Explanation: According to the passage, there is a government marketing board that takes care of selling the crops; this means that farmers might not know how to market their product. Furthermore, Levin argues that "the only way forward is an immediate halt to government-led price fixing." If Levin supports this action, it is logical that he would support training farmers to perform tasks that were handled by the government boards.

2. B

Explanation: Hogue "thinks that forcing Canadian farmers to compete with major players on the international open market discourages family farms, especially ones producing specialty crops or livestock varieties." Because of this, it's possible to turn this idea around and assume that specialty farmers would agree with Hogue.

Activity 5

Example notes; answers may vary.

VIEWPOINT 1 (TIM DIAMONTI)	VIEWPOINT 2 (EDU PSYC)	EXTRA VIEWPOINT (SPEAKER)
Formats good 4 learners No more paper materials Learner needs internet Computer = tutor ↑ communication/prof	Concerned → effects Eye strain Lazy Note-taking import. 4 understanding Interpersonal skill ↓	Space need ↓ E-book, journal enough E-journal helpful Meeting rooms = tech tools
TOPIC: Computers in education		

Test Practice

1. B
2. A
3. A
4. D
5. C
6. B

SPEAKING – UNIT 7

Activity 1

1. I **advise** you to review all the new words you learn each day.
2. I think you should take my **advice** about speaking French as much as you can outside of class.
3. Listen carefully: I have an important **piece of advice** for you.
4. My friends gave me a lot of **advice** when I first started learning a new language.
5. I have a friend who gave me some **advice** that I didn't find useful, so I **advise** you to study for this class in whatever way works for you!

Activity 2

Possible Answers

1. Why don't you finish eating a little before your break ends so you're not late getting back to work?
2. You had better check the flyers for sales and go shopping when there are good discounts.
3. You might want to offer computer skills training to the team.
4. Why not come out with me next week and meet some new people?
5. You should try to find a group that shares your hobbies or interests.
6. You had better not wear casual clothes when you go to the interview.
7. You could try making a list of new words and put them on your fridge.
8. Why don't you try changing the image in the logo?

Activity 3

Possible Answers

1. **Being Repetitive**
   - The test taker uses the word "just" six times. It would have been better for her to include other ways of expressing the same idea, such as "you only have to" or "simply."

2. **Confusing "Advice" with "Advise"**
   - The test taker said, "I'll **advice** you to just take bus from house to work." "Advice" is a noun. She should have used the verb "advise."

3. **Misusing Collocations**
   - The test taker said, "it will be faster than **having** a cab." The correct collocation is "**taking** a cab."
   - Later, the test taker said, "the job that you are going to transfer **with**." The correct collocation is to transfer **to**.

CELPIP Level Range: 7–8. This response may contain other types of errors, but this activity *only* focuses on the three types of errors mentioned in this section.

Rate the Response

SAMPLE RESPONSE 1
LEVELS: 5–6

Strengths
- Presents one solid piece of advice and includes some extra detail ("a toy store," "restaurant," stationery store," and "theatre").
- The vocabulary is general but is understandable. "Toy store," "famous restaurant," and "stationary" are accurate and support the message.

Weaknesses
- The stationary store and theatre ideas could have been better developed.
- Some of the vocabulary is simple and could have been better expressed ("the mall is very big").
- The phrase "her daughter" is repeated.
- There are errors in grammar ("there's a mall near in a apartment").
- Pauses and interjections break up the response and do not occur at natural points.

SAMPLE RESPONSE 2

LEVELS: 11–12

Strengths
- The response begins with more general ideas and then focuses on specific ideas and details.
- The transition from biking to activities on Toronto island is natural.
- Statements are well supported with extra details. For example, the expression "there's so many wonderful restaurants down Queen Street" is further supported by two extra pieces of information: "which is near where we live" and "where you are staying."
- Vocabulary is rich and accurate, which refine the meaning of the message.

Weaknesses
- None.

SAMPLE RESPONSE 3

LEVELS: 7–8

Strengths
- The response includes three suggestions.
- Suggestion about the CN Tower is well developed.
- The use of "food enthusiast" is extremely natural and contributes to the message.
- Word stress used for emphasis of important points.

Weaknesses
- The first two suggestions are under-developed compared to the third.
- Pauses detract slightly from coherence of the message.

SPEAKING – UNIT 8

Activity 1A
Possible Answers

Overview of the situation: changed opinion of colleague
What was the speaker's opinion? didn't like her
How did it change? colleague confided in her
Why did it change? realized colleague was going through personal issues
Resolution/Conclusion: good friends now

Activity 1B
Possible Answers

Overview of the situation: colleague helped teach speaker at new job
What was the speaker's opinion? (supporting detail): unapproachable, not nice, rude
How did it change? (supporting detail): colleague decided she could trust and talk to speaker
Why did it change? (supporting detail): got along better after discussing colleague's problems
Resolution/Conclusion: have coffee, lunch, dinner together now

Activity 2A
Answers will vary.
Note that the answers in this chart correspond to the high-level response in **Unit 8 – Track 2.**

Overview of the situation	seeing family again after 9 years abroad
Why were you at the airport?	returning home to visit family
Who were you with?	friend
Why do you remember that time?	best moment of life; excited to travel and see family again
Resolution/Conclusion	successfully travelled to see family

Activity 3A

1. The other day,
2. And then
3. a couple of days earlier

Activity 3B/3C

Note that the following time sequencers are accurate to this test taker's response. However, your answers for Activity 3B may be slightly different.

1. a couple of weeks ago
2. And then
3. Then
4. a couple of days later

Activity 4

Possible Answers

1. **Failing to Use Time Sequencers**
   - The test taker did not use time sequencers to help connect ideas in the response. For example, this makes it hard to know if the test taker was "happily waiting for her" at home while the sister was at camp, or while they were in the airport. To be more clear, the test taker could have said something like, "while my sister was collecting her luggage, we were happily waiting for her."

2. **Using Flat Intonation**
   - The response does not include a wide range of intonation. This makes it harder for the listener to understand how the speaker feels about his experience.
   - Since the response is generally flat, it is challenging to listen for key words as they have the same intonation as everything else. In comparison, higher-level speech has differences in intonation that make it easier to listen for important words and ideas.

3. **Using a Stop-and-Start Rhythm**
   - There are continuous starts and stops throughout the response. This makes it hard for the listener to follow the response, and they need to use more effort to understand what is being said.

CELPIP Level Range: 5–6. This response may contain other types of errors, but this activity *only* focuses on the three types of errors mentioned in this section.

Rate the Response

> **SAMPLE RESPONSE 1**
>
> **LEVELS: 5–6**
>
> **Strengths**
> - Speaker clearly states her decision at beginning of response.
> - Response includes plenty of details and reasons for why the choice was difficult (hard to see parents; what if there was an emergency; etc.).
> - Speaker attempts to use longer sentence structures.
> - Speaker clearly addresses each aspect of the instructions.
>
> **Weaknesses**
> - Speaker repeatedly mistakes verb tense ("when I **graduate** high school" instead of "when I **graduated** high school"; "my parents **will missing** me" instead of "my parents **would** miss me").
> - Response contains errors with article use ("come to **the** Canada" instead of "come to Canada").
> - Response contains multiple instances of repetition which may detract from listenability ("I'm 18 years old . . . I'm 18 years old"; "when I . . . when I graduate high school").

SAMPLE RESPONSE 2

LEVELS: 7–8

Strengths
- Speaker clearly states his decision at beginning of response.
- Speaker uses logical transitions and sequencing in response.
- Speaker uses advanced sentence structures.

Weaknesses
- Speaker's use of tense is often confusing ("right now, **I'm finishing** high school and I **needed** to decide . . ."; "I **was thinking** about it for 2 years now"—is he speaking about something in the past or the present?).
- Response includes some issues with word choice ("my mom **suggested me** something" instead of "my mom recommended that").
- Some imprecise word choices suggest speaker has limited vocabulary ("like, I never had a dream job or something").
- Speaker does not fully address instructions (did his decision turn out well?).

SAMPLE RESPONSE 3

LEVELS: 9–10

Strengths
- Speaker uses complex sentence structures.
- Speaker speaks for full time with very few pauses or interjections.
- Response includes numerous details to support why the decision was easy to make.
- Speaker fully addresses all aspects of task.

Weaknesses
- Meaning is sometimes unclear ("because the salary was much higher . . . there was a better standard of living"—can she clarify that this was on the new island, and not where she currently lived?).
- Speaker includes some repetition ("**make** the change **easier**" and "**made** the decision much **easier**"; "**in the end**, I have now been there 10 years, and **in the end**, I am very happy . . .").

SPEAKING – UNIT 9

Activity 1

- ✓ I see an office.
- ✓ There are seven people working in the office.
- ✓ They seem to be working on different tasks.

Activity 2

Possible Answers

1. on	4. on	7. Beside
2. beside	5. between	8. opposite
3. Next to	6. across from	

Activity 3

Possible Answers

1. **the woman in the light blue business suit**
2. the tall man in the burgundy sweater holding the papers
3. the man with spiky black hair talking on the phone
4. the man wearing blue headphones
5. the blond woman in front of the large whiteboard

Activity 4

1. playing with a truck	4. dancing together	7. leaning against a tree
2. sitting on the bench	5. doing a handstand	8. racing each other
3. playing Frisbee	6. posing for photos	9. having a water fight

Activity 5

Possible Answers

1. **The two short-haired boys in the sandbox are playing with a toy truck.**
2. The woman in the green shirt sitting on the bench is talking on the phone.
3. The man in the yellow shirt is playing Frisbee with the red-haired man.
4. The two young girls between the sandbox and the path are dancing together.
5. The tall man next to the two girls is doing a handstand.
6. The people on the checkered picnic blanket are posing for photos.
7. The man in the grey vest leaning against a tree is taking a selfie.
8. The cyclist in the black and green shirt and the woman in rollerblades are racing each other on the path.
9. The man and woman beside the path are having a water fight with colourful plastic guns.

Activity 6

Possible Answers

1. **Incorrect Word Choice**
   - The response includes a few instances of unclear word choice. For example, the speaker says "two kids in the ground" instead of "**dirt**" or "**sandbox.**" Also, the speaker describes a girl "sitting on a **desk**" instead of a "**bench.**" These incorrect word choices could confuse the listener, who cannot see the image.

2. **Misusing Verb Forms**
   - The speaker attempts to use present progressive tense, but they sometimes leave out the "be" verb, making the response more difficult to follow. For example, "they **playing** with a small car" instead of "they **are playing** with a small car" and "they **trying** to take from each other" instead of "they **are trying** to take [it] from each other."

3. **Using Incorrect Subject-Verb Agreement**
   - Many verbs in this response do not agree with the singular/plural nouns that they are referencing. This makes the number of people in the image less clear to the listener. For example, "there **is** two little **girl**" should be "there **are** two little **girls**"; "there's two girls" should be "**there are** two girls"; and "they are little **boy**" should be "they are little **boys**."

CELPIP Level Range: 5–6. This response may contain other types of errors, but this activity *only* focuses on the three types of errors mentioned in this section.

Rate the Response

SAMPLE RESPONSE 1
LEVELS: 5–6

Strengths
- The response covers the main elements in the image.
- The opening statement provides a clear overview of the image.
- Vocabulary is simple, but communicates the message.

Weaknesses
- The tense (past, present, future) is not well maintained throughout the response.
- The response demonstrates difficulties selecting the correct vocabulary, park -> backyard, naked -> shirtless.
- Pauses reduce cohesion and detract from listenability.

SAMPLE RESPONSE 2
LEVELS: 8–9

Strengths
- Good vocabulary ("skipping," "game on the sidewalk," "sun bath").
- Addresses all elements in the image.
- Pronunciation is clear and does not detract from the message.
- The rate of speech is neither too fast nor too slow.

Weaknesses
- The response lacks transitions between ideas.
- Pauses are not in natural positions as the speaker hunts for vocabulary.
- There is a lack of sentence variety in the response.

SAMPLE RESPONSE 3
LEVELS: 11–12

Strengths
- Good overview of the image.
- Vocabulary is well suited to the task ("get together," "collection").
- Grammar is accurate and varied.
- Pronunciation and intonation is natural.

Weaknesses
- None.

SPEAKING – UNIT 10

Activity 1

Possible Answers
1. The man holding the paper will probably place it back down.
2. The woman using a laptop is going to continue working on a graph.
3. The woman sitting by the whiteboard is going to make a plan with her colleague.
4. The man on the phone is about to make an important business deal.
5. The man wearing headphones will continue listening to his music.

Activity 2A

Possible Answers
1. The kids in the sandbox will fight over the toy car.
2. The woman sitting on the bench will finish her conversation on the phone.
3. The man about to catch the Frisbee is about to trip and fall over.
4. The girls dancing are going to continue to dance.
5. The man doing a handstand will land on his feet and smile proudly.
6. The people taking pictures are going to change their position for a new photo.
7. The man leaning against the tree is going to take a picture of himself with a phone.
8. The kids racing down the path are going to stop and catch their breath.
9. The man and woman having a water fight are going to splash the woman taking photos of her friends.

Activity 2B

Possible Answers
1. The kids in the sandbox are going to drive the car into the sandcastle.
2. The woman sitting on the bench will stand up and walk away.
3. The man about to catch the Frisbee will catch it and quickly throw it back to his friend.
4. The man leaning against the tree will eventually fall asleep.
5. The man and woman having a water fight will get very wet.
6. The kids racing down the path will crash into each other and fall on the grass.
7. The girls dancing will stop and begin playing tag.
8. The man doing a handstand will fall over and start laughing.
9. The people taking pictures will finish and leave.

Activity 3

Possible Answers

1. **Making Unrealistic Predictions**
   - The response focuses too much on "nice food in the restaurant" and what will happen after leaving the park. This is not directly based on information within the image. There is nothing in the image to suggest what might happen after the people leave the park, yet most of the response is focused on dinner, restaurants, and going home.

2. **Pausing**
   - The response includes numerous pauses. This frequency detracts from the clarity of the response. In particular, it is sometimes unclear whether these pauses indicate the end of an idea, or whether the speaker is continuing with the idea after each pause.

3. **Interjecting**
   - The speaker uses so many interjections that they sometimes impact the clarity of the response. It is harder to follow the logic of the speaker's ideas when his thoughts are interrupted by interjections.

CELPIP Level Range: 5–6. This response may contain other types of errors, but this activity *only* focuses on the three types of errors mentioned in this section.

Rate the Response

SAMPLE RESPONSE 1
LEVELS: 5–6

Strengths
- Good use of sentence variety ("the girl that is jumping on the street will lose her balance").
- The response provides reasons and details for each prediction.
- The response is generally delivered at a good rate of speech.

Weaknesses
- The response does not last the whole time.
- Long pauses detract from cohesion.
- Grammar errors are common, but do not cause problems with communicating the message.
- There is a lack of explanation to support the predictions in the response.

SAMPLE RESPONSE 2
LEVELS: 11–12

Strengths
- Good use of "I suspect" to indicate predictions.
- Good use of prepositions to show where people are in the image.
- Natural pace and pauses increase understandability of the response.

Weaknesses
- None.

SAMPLE RESPONSE 3
LEVELS: 9–10

Strengths
- There are no grammatical errors in the response.
- The pace and intonation are natural and enhance the response.
- All major elements in the image are addressed.

Weaknesses
- Only one reason for the predictions is presented in the response.
- The response provides a basic message focusing on one event rather than many events.
- Ideas are presented in a list with a small range of connecting words ("and," "and then," "and so," "but then").

SPEAKING – UNIT 11

Activity 1A

1. Strong

Explanation: This is a strong argument because it provides reasons to support the choice.

2. Weak

Explanation: This argument is weak because it is not clear what the advantage of the material (leather) is or whether the price is favourable. The following is an example of an improved version: I think we should buy the red jacket for Susan. It's made of leather, so it will last a long time, and $129.99 is a good price for a jacket of that quality; I've seen a similar jacket for much more.

3. Strong

Explanation: This is a strong argument because it provides reasons to support the choice.

4. Strong

Explanation: This is a strong argument because it provides reasons to support the choice.

5. Weak

Explanation: This argument is weak because it is not supported by any reasons—just factual statements. The following is an example of an improved version: I suggest that we stay at the hotel on Broadway. I've stayed there before, and it was quite comfortable and conveniently located. Also, there's a great restaurant in the lobby that makes delicious burgers!

Activity 1B

Possible Answers

1. I recommend that you rent the apartment instead of the basement suite because, even though the cost is the same, the apartment looks much nicer and it's located in a quieter neighbourhood.
2. We should definitely take the shuttle bus from the airport since it comes much more frequently than the train, and it's way cheaper than taking a taxi.

Activity 2

Answers will vary. The following notes are based on the assumption that the test taker has chosen the Sun Garden. However, Prince Edward Gardens is equally valid.

ADVANTAGES (YOUR CHOICE)	DISADVANTAGES (FIANCÉ'S FATHER'S CHOICE)
1. 2 acres– it's a large wedding, so plenty of room to wander around 2. Includes tea and Chinese cakes (maybe additional food for a fee?); this is all catered, so it should be really good 3. Sun Garden has beautiful gardens—great setting for wedding 4. If it rains, Sun Garden includes use of indoor housing; definitely large enough to accommodate everyone	• ¼ acre– it's a large wedding, so maybe not enough room to hold everyone • Family needs to cook—too much work—no one wants to cook on wedding day • It's only the backyard of a house, so it's not very elegant—not great for a wedding • If it rains, house probably won't be big enough to hold everyone, and it may not be clean . . .

Activity 3

1. more spacious than
2. more scenic
3. nicer
4. more expensive
5. better

Activity 4

Possible Answers

1. **Using Empty Phrases**
   - The test taker says "something like that" multiple times. This phrase is vague and does not contribute any useful information to his response. If he had avoided using this empty phrase, he would have had more time to support his choice with more meaningful phrases.

2. **Failing to Compare the Two Options**
   - The test taker does choose an option near the beginning of his response ("I can choice uhh, the Sun Garden"), but he never addresses what his fiancé's father wants, nor does he compare the two options against each other.

3. **Lacking Organized Structure**
   - The response switches between different examples ("quiet," "noisy," "Sun Garden's nice," "location is good") without explaining the reasons in much detail. This makes it difficult to follow the organization of ideas.

CELPIP Level Range: 5–6. This response may contain other types of errors, but this activity *only* focuses on the three types of errors mentioned in this section.

Rate the Response

SAMPLE RESPONSE 1
LEVELS: 5–6

Strengths
- The response presents a clear opinion.
- Comparisons between cost and travel time are made.
- There is a concluding statement.

Weaknesses
- The grammar has small errors such as "it's more expensive, it's 306 dollars, than the gas is . . . is 206 dollars."
- There are some issues with word choice such as "It will less the body ache."
- Pauses disrupt the flow of ideas when talking about the cost.
- No reference to departure time was made.

SAMPLE RESPONSE 2
LEVELS: 11–12

Strengths
- Good use of vocabulary ("gruelling").
- Natural rate of speech and intonation.
- The position is well explained and there are comparisons between all three points.

Weaknesses
- Some pauses, but they do not impact the message.

SAMPLE RESPONSE 3
LEVELS: 7–8

Strengths
- Natural comparisons of the information with good reasons ("I am not willing to sit 7 hours in a car").
- Spoke for the full time.
- Natural transitions and connections between ideas.
- The position is well expressed and is clear.

Weaknesses
- Did not make a concluding sentence.
- Some awkward phrases ("I think my choice to go").
- Repetition of words sometimes make it hard to understand the message.

SPEAKING – UNIT 12

<u>Activity 1</u>

1. **Direct Statement:** You must return the dog to the pet shop.
   a) **Polite Statement:** I'm sorry to bring this up, but you will need to return the dog to the pet shop.
   b) **Reason:** I have serious allergies to pets and can't breathe through my nose.

2. **Direct Statement:** You have to sell your car.
   a) **Polite Statement:** I feel really bad about this, but I think you should consider selling your car.
   b) **Reason:** The car insurance is quite expensive, and neither of us drives the car enough to justify the cost.

3. **Direct Statement:** You must quit your job.
   a) **Polite Statement:** I'm afraid to tell you this, but I think you should leave your job.
   b) **Reason:** It's really been stressing you out lately, and I think that's causing the health problems you've had these past few months.

4. **Direct Statement:** You can't go to work next week.
   a) **Polite Statement:** Would you consider taking next week off?
   b) **Reason:** I have to travel for my work, and there's no one else who can take care of the kids during that time.

5. **Direct Statement:** You have to sign up for an exercise class.
   a) **Polite Statement:** Would you be willing to join an exercise class?
   b) **Reason:** You've been so tired lately, and I think more exercise would help to boost your energy.

6. **Direct Statement:** I'm quitting your yoga class.
   a) **Polite Statement:** Sorry for the inconvenience, but I need to leave your yoga class.
   b) **Reason:** I will be moving to a new city at the end of the week and won't be able to attend anymore.

<u>Activity 2A</u>

Answers will vary.

- Big company
- New employees
- Very upset
- Your department
- Smaller
- Other side of the office
- Colder

<u>Activity 2B</u>

Answers will vary.

<u>**Excuse me, I was wondering if we could talk about the planned departmental move. I'm not sure moving is the best idea**</u> because the space on the other side of the office is much smaller than our current space, and it's also way too cold over there all the time. If we have to work in cramped conditions, this may lead to interpersonal conflict, and being too cold may even negatively impact our health. In fact, one of my colleagues is so upset by this that he's considering quitting.

<u>**Also, if we move,**</u> this may disrupt our productivity. Sure, it may only take a day or two to move our desks and office supplies and so on, but this is still time that we could better spend finishing our various projects. In comparison, if the new employees were put on the other side of the office, they'd still be going through orientation and training anyway, so there would be no loss in productivity.

<u>**Finally, I believe it's best if we**</u> stay where we are because this would help with morale. Everyone in our department has been with the company for quite a while, and moving us may imply that we are not very important to the company. But if we remain where we are, this will demonstrate that we are important to the company, and everyone will be happy! Thank you!

Activity 2C

Possible Answers

- There are ways to stay warm: USB heated seat, quilt
- Bigger windows, good view, more sunlight
- Get more comfortable chairs
- The job market is not great

Activity 3

Possible Answers

1. **Failing to Address the Listener Directly**
   - The speaker begins her response by talking **about** her co-worker, rather than **to** her co-worker ("I think **my co-worker** . . . shouldn't . . . quit because . . . I try to convince **him**.").
   - The speaker does not directly address her co-worker (the listener, in this case) until the end of the response.
   - This shift from talking **about** the listener to talking **to** the listener could be confusing, and her introduction is not a good use of time. If the speaker had immediately addressed her co-worker directly, she could have saved time.

2. **Expressing Incomplete Ideas**
   - The response contains many instances of incomplete ideas. For instance, the speaker begins with "I think my co-worker, um, shouldn't be quit because, um I try to convince him because . . ." This could be confusing to the listener, as the first "because" leads us to expect a reason, which we don't get. Instead, it is unclear if the speaker attempts to rephrase her statement, or whether she moves straight on to a new idea.
   - The statement "The bosses are good from here, and the same as all that like the employ the co-workers . . ." would likely be very confusing to the listener. It is unclear what the speaker means about the bosses, and the shift from "employ" (possibly "employees") to "co-workers" is also confusing. It seems that multiple ideas are being discussed here, but none of them appear to be fully developed.

3. **Using Words in the Wrong Order**
   - The speaker sometimes mistakes the order of words in her response.
   - For example, the speaker says "and the most probably thing that I like" instead of "and probably the thing that I like the most . . ."

CELPIP Level Range: 7–8. This response may contain other types of errors, but this activity *only* focuses on the three types of errors mentioned in this section.

Rate the Response

SAMPLE RESPONSE 1
LEVELS: 3–4

Strengths
- The position in the response is clear.
- Good details are used to support ideas.
- The response uses an appropriate tone for the audience.

Weaknesses
- Struggles with pronunciation ("suggestion").
- Grammar contains errors ("can you notice your voice").
- The response confuses the task because it implies that Albert is the neighbour, not the roommate.

SAMPLE RESPONSE 2
LEVELS: 7–8

Strengths
- The position is very clear.
- Suggestions such as "use ear plugs" provide detail.
- Stress and intonation are natural and support the message.

Weaknesses
- Expressions such as "okay Bonnie, you need to understand" and "you have to deal with the problems" are aggressive.
- Some grammatical errors such as "natural loud voice" and "in a good manner" detract from the message.

SAMPLE RESPONSE 3
LEVELS: 11–12

Strengths
- The response contains strong details such as "Natural feature of his personality."
- Pronunciation is natural and enhances the message.
- The position in the response is clear and all details focus on the message.
- The tone of the response is appropriate to the task.

Weaknesses
- The response lacks a summarizing statement or conclusion.

SPEAKING – UNIT 13

Activity 1

1. I believe that
2. As far as I'm concerned
3. In my opinion
4. In my experience
5. I'd say that
6. Personally, I think that

Activity 2A

GIVING EXAMPLES/ CLARIFYING	for instance	in other words	for example	specifically
SEQUENCING	yet while	finally	first	to begin with
CAUSE/EFFECT	since because	therefore hence	consequently	if . . . then
ADDING INFORMATION	not only . . . but also		moreover	
EXPRESSING SIMILARITY	both . . . and		similarly	
CONTRAST	however on the one hand . . . on the other hand	but	whereas	in comparison

Activity 2B

Answers will vary.

1. because/since
2. not only . . . but also
3. both . . . and
4. however / in comparison
5. On the one hand . . . on the other hand

Activity 3

1. know
2. knowledge
3. known
4. knowing

Activity 4

Answers will vary. This response demonstrates multiple forms of each key word presented in the activity.

I think that governments should pay for free post-secondary education for all their citizens. In many countries, tuition at colleges and universities is very costly, and let's face it . . . most students don't have much in their bank accounts. When you add in the cost of textbooks, and other educational materials, and accommodations if you're from out of town, many students just can't afford to pursue higher learning.

If you talk to someone who is attending university or college, they will often tell you that the only way they can afford it is by taking out student loans for which they will be making payments for years after they graduate. But if the government paid for everyone's tuition, I think this would allow more students to attend. And the higher the attendance rate at colleges and universities, the more highly educated graduates will enter the workforce, and the nation's economy will benefit a lot. At first glance, free tuition might seem like it will end up costing a lot for the government, but I believe that this increase to the workforce would more than balance whatever the government spends on funding post-secondary studies.

Activity 5

Possible Answers

1. **Missing Uncountable Nouns**
   - The test taker says "putting **garbages**" instead of "**garbage**." "Garbage" is an uncountable noun and, as such, does not have a plural form.

2. **Failing to Provide Strong Reasons for Opinion**
   - The test taker mainly discusses how individual citizens can help reduce pollution, but some of these examples do not make complete sense. For example, she does not fully explain how "cleaning up our houses" or cleaning up garbage will directly impact air or water pollution.
   - These examples also do not fully explain why the test taker has the opinion that citizens should help reduce pollution; they mainly explain how it can be reduced.

3. **Failing to Follow All Instructions**
   - The test taker spends much of the response discussing how to reduce noise pollution. However, noise pollution was not mentioned in the task instructions. Instead, the test taker should have read the instructions more carefully and focused on why citizens should help reduce air and water pollution (these are mentioned in the instructions, but they are not specifically mentioned in the response).

CELPIP Level Range: 5–6. This response may contain other types of errors, but this activity *only* focuses on the three types of errors mentioned in this section.

Rate the Response

SAMPLE RESPONSE 1
LEVELS: 5–6
Strengths
• Clear opening statement that provides a position.
• Ideas and supporting details are on topic.
• Good use of vocabulary such as "appropriate."
Weaknesses
• Some phrases are awkward ("it depends from where they are," "especially through online").
• Pauses reduce cohesion.

SAMPLE RESPONSE 2
LEVELS: 11–12
Strengths
• Strong use of details and reasons to support position.
• Ideas connect logically to each other.
• Effective vocabulary selection contributes to the development of the message.
Weaknesses
• Errors in grammar occur, especially subject/verb agreement ("afterward we become friend").
• Use of varied and figurative language is not sustained throughout the response.

SAMPLE RESPONSE 3
LEVELS: 9–10
Strengths
• Good use of rhetorical questions ("do I think he is a very good man?").
• Good use of details (5 specific details/examples).
• Speaks for the entire time.
• Pronunciation is clear and supports the message.
Weaknesses
• Errors in grammar occur, but do not detract from understanding the message.

SPEAKING – UNIT 14

Activity 1

Possible Answers

1. Street lamp
   a) Simple Description: *large light on a metal pole*
   b) Detailed Description: *street lamp with a fluted bottom and a large bulb in a decorative casing*
2. Cart/Carriage
   a) Simple Description: open car with benches on wheels
   b) Detailed Description: bright green carriage with open sides and four grey benches
3. Cart roof/top
   a) Simple Description: green and white roof/top
   b) Detailed Description: cheerful green-, red-, and white-striped top with scalloped edges
4. Driver
   a) Simple Description: the man in the open car
   b) Detailed Description: costumed driver with a moustache, wearing a green cap and red tie
5. Megaphone
   a) Simple Description: thing that makes your voice louder
   b) Detailed Description: medium-sized white megaphone with a red handle
6. Saddles
   a) Simple Description: red seat on the horses
   b) Detailed Description: simple red saddle with a grey pommel

Activity 2B

TRACK 1	TRACK 2
• *corner store has vegetable and fruits*	• a corner store that basically sell fresh produce like fruit and vegetables • some of the vendors, the people selling the fruit and the vegetables
• *outside the city street*	• a farm, like rural area • *a place where farmers would live*
• the sign "Fresh Fruits"	• *a big banner that says "Fresh Fruits" on my left-hand side*
• *another building in front of the corner store* • *with red roof*	• another place that looks like a diner or a restaurant

Activity 3A

Possible notes

QUESTIONS TO ASK YOURSELF	NOTES				
Who am I talking to?	*Jamie, niece*				
Are there any people?	*No*				
Is the scene inside or outside?	*Outside*				
What is the season?	*Spring/Summer*				
What is the time of day in the picture?	*Daytime*				
What is/are the main object(s) used for?	*Exercise*	*Entertainment*		*Playground equipment*	
What shape(s) is/are the main object(s)?	*Curves*	*Lots of shapes*			
What colour(s) is/are the main object(s)?	*Black*	*Grey*	*Silver*	*Orange (handholds)*	*Green (steps)*
What is/are the main object(s)?	*Two standing areas on rails with handles*			*Standing area with ring*	
What is/are the material(s)?	*Metal - rails*	*Rubber – rings to stand on at ends of device*			

<u>Activity 3B</u>
1. "it looks like a couple of **chairs**"; "almost like a little **roller coaster**"
2. "picture, like, a **hammock** that's supported by two poles"

<u>Activity 4</u>
Possible Answers
1. **Misusing Prepositions**
   - The response contains multiple instances of incorrect prepositions. Frequent misuse of prepositions can slow down the listener's ability to follow the response.
   - "I was running **on** the park" instead of "I was running **in** the park"
   - the [municipality] put it **on** the park" instead of "the [municipality] put it **in** the park"
   - "what we play **in**" instead of "what we play **on**"

2. **Going Off Topic**
   - The test taker says "It's very common, I think it's very common in this area and you saw more frequently." This statement does not satisfy the task instructions because it does not contribute to a physical description of the playground equipment. If the test taker had avoided going off topic like this, they would have had a bit more time to more accurately describe the equipment.
   - It is okay to use your imagination to help describe the situation, but *only* if this helps to address the task instructions. In this instance, the test taker's explanation does not help.

3. **Using Imprecise Language**
   - The test taker gives only vague descriptions of the playground equipment ("quite big equipment," "quite the oval," "it looks like something you would jump on," etc.). There is little to no description of specific aspects of the equipment. Using more precise language would have helped clarify this description for the listener.
   - For example, instead of "quite the oval," the test taker could have said, "This playground equipment looks like a set of monkey bars, some of which are shaped in an oval pattern."

CELPIP Level Range: 5–6. This response may contain other types of errors, but this activity *only* focuses on the three types of errors mentioned in this section.

<u>**Rate the Response**</u>

SAMPLE RESPONSE 1
LEVELS: 5–6

Strengths
- Provides good explanation of some parts of the umbrella.
- The response addressed both parts of the task.
- Delivery of message was natural and easy to understand.

Weaknesses
- Some grammatical errors such as "the picture of the whale and it's sprinkle the water on top" can lead to comprehension issues.
- The response did not describe all parts of the umbrella equally.

SAMPLE RESPONSE 2
LEVELS: 11–12

Strengths
- Good attempt at describing the umbrella without knowing the right word "Just like the glass mirrors on the church . . ."
- Pauses are natural and provide emphasis which enhances meaning.
- The description of each umbrella is complete and well presented.

Weaknesses
- Vocabulary is imprecise at times ("glass mirror" instead of "glass window," "dolphin" instead of "whale").
- Some grammar is inaccurate ("I know you like the yellow colour").

SAMPLE RESPONSE 3

LEVELS: 7–8

Strengths

- The response addressed both parts of the task.
- Good description of four of the umbrellas.
- Some good vocabulary like "rainbow," "monkey," "cartoon," and "characteristics."

Weaknesses

- Grammar issues detract slightly from the message ("one of the umbrella on the left is a blue one with whale on it").
- Pauses and repetition detract from the clarity of the message.